Teachers of tl

speeches and lectures by C........ ......ps

Bishop Alan Clark

Cardinal Cahal Daly

Cardinal Basil Hume

Cardinal Joseph Ratzinger

Bishop James Sangu

Cardinal Johannes Willebrands

Cardinal Thomas Winning

Archbishop Derek Worlock

Foreword by Cardinal Cormac Murphy-O'Connor

Edited by Tom Horwood

CATHOLIC BISHOPS' CONFERENCE OF ENGLAND AND WALES

ISBN 0 905241 19 3

Printed by MPG Books Ltd, Bodmin, Cornwall

CONTENTS

FOREWORD

The Second Vatican Council states that 'through the Holy Spirit who has been given to them, bishops have been made true and authentic teachers of the faith' (*Christus Dominus*, n. 2).

As 'shepherds' and successors to the Apostles, the bishops are charged with teaching and safeguarding the Catholic faith. They do this in communion with the Pope and in communion with each other.

This book brings together nine texts by well-known and well-loved bishops, fulfilling this commission to teach with clarity and authority. Although all were delivered in Britain over twenty-six years, the fact that many of the authors come from overseas demonstrates the unique and universal nature of the Body of Christ.

Each of the subjects addressed are crucial concerns for the Church at the beginning of the third Christian millennium. These powerful contributions to the Church's voice in our society deserve renewed study and, I am sure, will stimulate deep reflection.

Cardinal Cormac Murphy-O'Connor
Archbishop of Westminster

INTRODUCTION

The purpose of this book is to bring to a wider audience a few of the episcopal texts that have appeared in the pages of *Briefing* over the last quarter-century. *Briefing* has been the official documentation service of the Bishops' Conference of England and Wales since 1974, and of the Bishops' Conference of Scotland since 1988.

Many of the hundreds of documents and addresses from the Catholic Church in Britain and overseas that have appeared in *Briefing* had a particular relevance at the time they were published. Others, for instance those from the Holy See, are still available elsewhere. These nine addresses by individual bishops have been selected because they still resonate particularly strongly today. All were delivered in Britain. Together they represent some of the concerns and challenges facing the Church at the end of the twentieth century and at the beginning of the twenty-first - ranging from ecumenism and interfaith dialogue to international justice and peace, from education and ethics to spirituality. The names and positions of the authors indicate the great authority with which they speak.

Bishop James Sangu (1920-1998) was Bishop of Mbeya in Tanzania from 1966 to 1996. As Chairman of the Tanzanian Bishops' Conference, he was invited to speak at the annual conference of the Commission for International Justice and Peace of the Bishops' Conference of England and Wales in October 1975. Although some of the issues he refers to are now no longer principal concerns - apartheid, for example - his passionate address highlights many issues relating to the west's attitudes to aid and development that are still important.

Bishop Alan Clark (born 1919) was the Auxiliary Bishop of Northampton from 1969 to 1976, and then first Bishop of the new

7

Diocese of East Anglia until his retirement in 1994. Throughout his episcopal ministry, he was deeply involved in the dialogue aiming at Christian unity, most notably as Catholic co-Chairman of the Anglican/Roman Catholic International Commission (ARCIC) from 1969 to 1982. In 1974, he was the first Catholic bishop to address the Church of England General Synod. As well as providing an interesting background to subsequent ecumenical dialogue, his Cardinal Heenan Memorial Lecture of November 1978 focuses on the goal of Christian unity but does not shirk from recognising the sources of division between churches and ecclesial communities. Many of the issues are as relevant now as they were then.

Cardinal Cahal Brendan Daly (born 1917) is well known for his denunciations of violence in Northern Ireland. He was ordained Bishop of Ardagh and Clonmacnois in 1967, installed as Bishop of Down and Connor in 1982, and as Archbishop of Armagh and Primate of All Ireland in 1990. He was appointed cardinal the following year, and retired in 1996. His powerful address in September 1979 at a conference organised by the Bishops' Conference, CAFOD, the Catholic Institute for International Relations and Pax Christi was delivered a few days after the murder of Lord Mountbatten. For many years, the Church in Britain has prayed for peace and reconciliation in Northern Ireland. Cardinal Daly's arguments for a political solution to a political problem are fascinating in the light of the discussions in recent years following the Good Friday Agreement.

Cardinal Daly's other text, delivered at the Linacre Centre's twentieth anniversary conference in July 1997, witnesses to another of his particular concerns: today's moral crisis in the area of human life itself. Cardinal Daly has written extensively on moral philosophy and natural law. Here he examines the role of the Church's teaching in the face of the challenge of what Pope John Paul II has referred to as the growing 'culture of death'.

Cardinal Johannes Willebrands (born 1909) was President of the Pontifical Council for Promoting Christian Unity from 1969 to 1989. He was ordained bishop in 1964, created cardinal in 1969, and was also Archbishop of Utrecht from 1975 to 1983. In March 1985, Cardinal Willebrands spoke at the Oxford Union on the alleged anti-Semitism of Christianity, addressing the subject from the perspective of Christian interpretations of the New Testament culminating in the challenging vision of the Second Vatican Council.

Cardinal Joseph Ratzinger (born 1927), was Archbishop of Munich-Freising from 1977 to 1982. He was created cardinal in 1977, and has been Prefect of the Congregation for the Doctrine of the Faith since 1981. His Fisher Lecture at Cambridge University in January 1988 argues strongly for morality and faith at a time of increasing materialism.

Archbishop Derek Worlock (1920-1996) was Bishop of Portsmouth from 1965 to 1976, and then Archbishop of Liverpool. As secretary to successive Cardinal Archbishops of Westminster, he had been involved at the centre of the Church hierarchy for many years. Education is one of the most covered topics in the pages of *Briefing*, but most the texts have been very specifically focused on particular pieces of legislation or events. Archbishop Worlock's anecdotal address to the Catholic Education Conference in April 1995 takes a broader view, relating the circumstances behind the momentous Education Act of 1944. It is an important reminder of the struggle the Church had to establish the national provision for Catholic schools that can so easily be taken for granted today. The struggle of the 1940s is also an indication that the principle of paying to safeguard Catholic ethos has been both a financial burden and a political lever.

Before becoming Archbishop of Westminster and cardinal in 1976, George Basil Hume OSB (1923-1999) was Abbot of the Benedictine Abbey at Ampleforth. Cardinal Hume was one of the best-loved churchmen of his generation. He was President of the Bishops' Conference of England and Wales from 1979 to 1999. In his De Lubac Lecture on 'Jesus Christ today', delivered in Salford in February 1998, he reflected on his own personal spiritual journey. At the dawn of a new century and millennium, he urges a reawakening of the spiritual instinct which is within everyone.

When Cardinal Thomas Winning died two years to the day after Cardinal Hume, on 17 June 2001, Cardinal Cormac Murphy-O'Connor paid tribute to his 'humour, dedication, utter loyalty, and unstinting defence of the Catholic Church'. The popular Scottish church leader was born in 1925, ordained priest in 1948 and Auxiliary Bishop of Glasgow in 1971. In 1974 he became Archbishop of Glasgow. He was President of the Bishops' Conference of Scotland from 1985, and was created cardinal in 1994. His Gonzaga Lecture at St Aloysius' College, Glasgow, in April 2001, sets out a wide-ranging agenda for the Church at the beginning of the twenty-first century, covering issues of inculturation and evangelisation, holiness, community, and the importance of the Eucharist.

As this unique anthology of texts from *Briefing* is published, it is appropriate to acknowledge all those who have been editors (and Scottish associate editors) over the years: the late Mgr Tom Connelly, Bishop Kieran Conry, Mgr James Hook, Peter Kearney, the late Mgr George Leonard, Fr Danny McLoughlin, David Miles Board, Patrick Olivier and Canon Peter Verity. For assistance and support with this project, thanks are particularly due to Margaret Smart and Fr Andrew Summersgill, and the authors and their estates.

Tom Horwood
Editor, Briefing

Bishop James Sangu (1975)
JUSTICE IN THE AFRICAN CONTEXT

Some time ago during the year I received a letter from your
Secretary General inviting me to address the Annual Conference of
the Commission for International Justice and Peace of the Bishops'
Conference of England and Wales. He indicated that the purpose of
this annual conference would be as follows:

> *To stimulate already fairly committed Christians to a deeper level of*
> *commitment and action for justice; to hear what an outsider thinks our*
> *priorities should be; to deepen our insight about what we can learn*
> *from the third world, and, in this case, Tanzania.*

To tell you the truth I received this invitation with mixed feelings.
First of all, a feeling of gratitude in giving me the honour. This is the
first time in my life to address a British audience. Secondly, a feeling
of apprehension, for although we are brothers in one faith, I cannot
help feeling I am a stranger, or as your Secretary put it in his letter,
an 'outsider' in your midst. Thirdly, I remembered the words of the
Synod of 1971 which declared that 'anyone who ventures to speak
to people about justice must first be just in their eyes'. These are
terrifying words. Happily I didn't venture!

On the other hand, to get the chance to talk to a sympathetic
audience like yours about justice, and especially about justice in the
African context, is a unique opportunity to strengthen our common
efforts to bring about greater justice in the world, and improve
relations between the churches in the old world and the young
churches in Africa.

To talk on justice. What an easy subject to talk on, but at the same
time what a complex subject; it all depends on the kind of audience.

Africa today

As you all know very well, Africa is going through a very crucial period in its history. Only decades ago, most African countries were colonies of western countries, among them Britain. In a rather short time almost all African countries have gained their independence and have become self-governing nations and members of the world family of nations.

The period of colonisation and the occupation of our countries by the western powers has by no means been an unadulterated blessing from the African point of view, although in the western press it has been hailed always as such, namely, to bring civilisation to the barbarous savages. African historians view this period from a completely different angle than European historians who all too often had to invent a justification for their intrusion in the African continent.

The process of decolonisation and the attainment of nationhood has put Africa in a very critical position. Many countries moved rapidly from tribal societies to nationhood, over-riding the former tribal sentiments and loyalties. This rapid transition from tribalism to nationalism has not always been easy and without conflict. There are many examples in Africa that especially larger tribes within one nation struggled fiercely to become the dominant force in the new nations. This struggle has been very clear, for instance, in Kenya, Nigeria, Congo, Burundi, Sudan, and is raging ferociously at present in Angola. This inter-tribal struggle for power is often immensely complicated by the interference of foreign powers who favour one or other tribe which they wish to use for their own political and economic interests. Africa becomes the battleground for foreign powers who wish to extend their sphere of influence in Africa, each providing an abundance of arms to their favourites, thereby enabling them to kill each other mercilessly.

Freedom

In the 1950s and 1960s a strong wind was blowing throughout the whole of Africa: the desire to attain freedom from the colonists. This cry for freedom, for independence, for human dignity, and the rejection of colonialism, foreign occupation, oppression and exploitation by the Europeans, becomes enormously strong. After having experienced for centuries crude slavery and later serfdom under the colonial governments, all the Africans wanted to shake off their shackles. They do not want any longer to be dominated by others; they cannot bear any longer to be considered by Europeans as savages, primitives, inferior human beings, peoples without civilisation or culture. To understand the rebellion against Europeans – often hate against Europeans – you have to imagine what it means to be told that you have no culture, no intelligence, that you are apes just climbing down from the trees, in all respects inferior to Europeans; to be treated as dumb servants, or at best with an air of condescension or in a patronising manner. In this way we Africans have been treated and are often still treated.

But the Africans have become convinced again that they are human beings, inferior to none. Perhaps poorer than Europeans, maybe less technically advanced, but nevertheless no less human than any other human race. For this reason the Africans want to be free, to regain their human dignity and self-respect. For this reason they cannot bear any longer that Africans remain under foreign domination in their own home. For this reason practically all African countries support the liberation movements of those countries under foreign domination, and peace will not come to Africa until this thorn in the flesh is eradicated in the whole of the continent.

Rhodesia

Since the decolonisation of the Portuguese territories there remain only a few countries which have not yet attained independence, most prominent among them Namibia and Rhodesia. Particularly in Rhodesia, Britain is closely involved. It is difficult to exaggerate the resentment many Africans have against Britain. Since the *Unilateral Declaration of Independence* of Rhodesia, Britain seems to have resigned herself that there is little she can do to help the Africans obtain their freedom. The suspicion among Africans is very strong that Britain really does not care about the fate and rights of the Africans, and that they are secretly more sympathetic to the fate of the handful of Europeans there, mainly of British origin, than in the fate of millions of Africans. Last year, the bishops of Rhodesia protested strongly against the oppression of the Africans by the Rhodesian government. Recently the Commission for Justice and Peace of Rhodesia published here in England a report entitled *The Man in the Middle* documenting the cruelties and persecution committed by the Rhodesian illegal government, and describing how the African is the man in the middle between the hammer and the anvil. Bishop Lamont, President of the Commission for Justice and Peace in Rhodesia, writes in the introduction to the report, that as long as this situation continues, the Zimbabwean people will be irresistibly drawn to the communists, because they have nothing to lose. The conditions in Rhodesia are ideal to provoke violence, to destroy any hope for peaceful settlement, and finally to create a fertile soil for a Marxist or Maoist ideology.

His analysis is all too realistic as we have seen in other parts of Africa which are gradually falling under communist influence, because they seem to be sympathetic and helpful for the African struggle for freedom, whereas Christian western countries continue in their role of oppressor, indifferent spectator often gloating over African governments who fail to handle their newly gained independence efficiently.

But Britain cannot wash its hands of Rhodesia, and cannot escape its involvement in what is happening to the Africans there. Many people are of the opinion that the Rhodesian affair could have been solved earlier if the Christians of Britain had roused the conscience of their people and their government to end this injustice in Rhodesia, just as the independence of Mozambique has been hastened by the outcry of missionaries and Christians in Portugal against their government's colonial policy.

Obsession

Another case is South Africa. Its crude racialism is a continuous insult to all black Africans. It not only keeps the races apart, as it claims, but it shouts from the roofs the superiority of the white race and the inferiority of the black race. South Africa is an obsession for the Africans, and as long as this situation continues, there is really little chance that the black Africans will ever live in brotherhood with white Europeans. And here again, Britain has close ties with South Africa and many vested interests. Because of these interests she prefers to keep quiet about the indignities the Africans have to suffer. They appear to be interested, not in justice, but in their investments and economic interests. The often used excuse that sports has nothing to do with politics, that business has nothing to do with politics, is vain. Politics has everything to do with economics, and is often based more on financial interests than moral principles. Some of the churches in South Africa oppose the racialist policies of the South African government, but their voice would gain in strength if they would get the support of the Christians in western countries. Notwithstanding the half-hearted denunciation of racialism by the western countries, South Africa feels strong because she is convinced of the backing she receives from the western countries, and because of the strong economic ties she has with these countries. As Christians we must fight for justice for the oppressed, not for financial gain and economic interest.

The colonialism of the recent past and the remnants which still exist in some parts of Africa up till now, is one of the reasons why Africans often have such strong anti-European feelings, and are rather easily attracted to communist countries which have no colonial past in Africa. Instead of peaceful and friendly relations between Africans and Europeans, we often notice feelings of antagonism, suspicion and even hatred, because the Africans feel that they have been ill-treated by the Europeans in the past, and because the Europeans still look down on them as inferior human beings.

Western exploitation

Listening to the voices of the third world, one often notices the harsh criticism of the west, and of the rich and developed countries. Peace is not only the absence of war, but the existence of friendly relations. In this sense we can hardly say that the third world is at peace with the western world. Notwithstanding the development aid given by the western countries, the third world often feels that she is not justly or fairly treated by the western world, but that she is still exploited, manipulated, dominated by the powerful nations which can impose their will on the poorer nations as they like. They use their power, their technical superiority, their riches, to force, often subtly, sometimes rudely, the poorer nations to accept their political views. Aid is often used as a kind of blackmail, and is given under conditions that the receiving country pays back by their unquestioning loyalty to the donor country. I could mention many examples. For instance, when Tanzania protested against the way Britain was handling the Rhodesian affair, Britain suspended her aid programme thereby wrecking Tanzania's first five-year development plan. When Tanzania refused to close the East German Consulate in Zanzibar, West Germany cancelled all its aid.

But apart from this misuse of aid to under-developed countries as a stick to keep them in line, there is a more fundamental issue which pitches the third world against the west. In international affairs, and in international trade, the developing countries are almost completely at the mercy of the developed countries. These fix the rules of the game, and the rules are fixed in such a way that they serve the interests of the rich countries. The poorer countries have simply to follow the rules imposed by the west.

You may sometimes wonder why the African countries, which have in the past suffered so much from the Arab slave trade, gave such wholehearted support to the Arab oil embargo, and the tremendous price increase in oil. One of the reasons is that the Arabs, reckoned among the under-developed countries, have been able just for once to impose their will on the western countries. Many of the developing countries, which supply raw materials to the west, would be only too happy if they could do the same thing.

During the last UNCTAD conference it was said repeatedly that the world economic order and the monetary system, devised and controlled by the great powers, is aimed at further enriching the already rich countries, thereby widening the gap between the poor and the rich countries. Is this right? Is this a practice of justice? Is it difficult to understand that such a situation necessarily provokes rebellion and threatens peace?

One cannot say that the riches of the world are justly divided among nations. One can point out easily how this situation has emerged, and which factors have produced this situation of utter inequality. But explaining the historical reasons does not justify the existence of this situation. The Pope has repeatedly accused this situation, and has said that it is the greatest world problem at the moment, and a dangerous threat to world peace. This situation has prompted the Vatican Council to establish the Commission for International Justice and Peace. This situation has to be changed, and it will have to be changed primarily by those countries which have the power to change it, and those are the rich countries.

It has become a common understanding in recent years that peace without justice is impossible. Peace can only be obtained in a situation where justice is done to everybody. Nobody has the right to demand that the suffering and the oppressed keep quiet and accept unquestioningly their lot.

African injustice to Africans

Looking at Africa you could well ask me the question, is justice done to the Africans by Africans? First of all we have to notice the fact that a lot of injustices are committed to Africans by Africans themselves. This problem was stated very clearly by our President Nyerere, when he explained why he could not attend in good conscience the last OAU meeting in Kampala. I quote:

> The people of Africa are fighting for human dignity, for equality, and the right to live in freedom. It is not surprising that the whole of Africa cries out against the atrocities of the colonial and racist states. The strong and public outcry from Africa is justified, correct and necessary. But when massacres, oppression and torture are used against Africans in the independent African states there is no protest from anywhere in Africa. There is silence even when such crimes are perpetrated by or with the connivance of African governments and the leaders of African states. Africa is in danger of becoming unique in its refusal to protest about the crimes committed against Africans, provided such actions are done by African leaders and African governments. By this attitude we are undermining the validity of Africa's demand that justice and equality and dignity should prevail in southern Africa, and wherever people of African descent are discriminated against on grounds of their colour.

As President Nyerere pointed out in his statement: there is an awful lot of injustice committed in Africa by the Africans themselves.

He includes our own country by saying: 'We are not claiming that Tanzania has a record of unfailing rectitude in matters of human rights; we are only too conscious of our many failures in this respect.' Injustices are committed in Africa by Africans and this causes us acute embarrassment. It may be adduced as a reason to deny Africans the right to decry the injustices committed to the Africans by others. You could tell me to speak about justice to my fellow Africans first before speaking to you. It is clear that we, the Church in Africa, have the Christian duty to accuse our own people and our own governments of the injustices committed by them. And I may state that this is exactly what we are doing, although perhaps not always forcefully enough. But I could point out many churches and church leaders who have come into conflict with their governments exactly because they oppose oppressive policies, and decry injustices committed by these governments.

Besides the injustices committed to Africans by Africans, African peoples suffer injustices inflicted on them by the western world. I have indicated already some of them: continued colonialism in Rhodesia and Namibia; crude racialism in South Africa; abuse of internal conflicts by western and eastern powers; the use of aid with political strings attached. But the basic issue which pitches the third world against the western world is the unjust world order which results in the fact that the gap between the poor and rich countries continues to widen instead of diminishing. The powerful and developed countries dominate the world, not only militarily and politically, but also economically. They dictate the world market; they dominate the world monetary system. Their capitalism is geared not towards justice for all, but towards their own profits. Business is business, it is said. In practice this often means that as long as you make a profit for your own purse it does not matter that you plunder others.

Western standards

When you look at the actions of the various western governments, it appears that they are scared to death of policies which might lower a little the standard of living of their own people, but they do not really care about the destitution of millions upon millions outside their borders. It means that governments and politicians are almost intrinsically selfish; that is, they care for the people who elected them, but they hardly care about far-off nations. This narrow nationalism is intolerable in the present world, and it is definitely un-Christian. How often have world problems been discussed in international conferences? Everybody agrees that the extreme inequality between the poor and the rich nations is not right, that it must be corrected. But when it comes down to practical conclusions almost every government walks out, because they cannot sell these propositions to their voters. Governments follow their voters. Unless the voters undergo a change of heart and are dedicated to the establishment of international justice rather than their own comfort the present horrible situation will continue.

Price fixing

When the Arabs raised oil prices without consulting the consumer countries, the western world cried out, 'foul play'. Don't they realise that they have been doing the same thing to the under-developed countries for the last century? The under-developed countries have to supply the raw materials to the industrialised world at minimum prices, and they have to buy the finished products at high prices.

Most under-developed countries would be only too happy if they themselves could fix the prices of their raw materials in such a way that it would provide their own people with a decent standard of living. But they do not dare to do it yet; they would kill themselves economically. If Zambia refused to sell her copper under a certain price which is not acceptable to the industrialised countries, it would be bankrupt in no time. It has to sell, if she wishes to survive, at any price the consumer countries dictate. The only way for the under-developed countries is to accept the market rules of the industrialised countries, although they do it reluctantly because they are forced, not because they are convinced it is just and fair.

Recently President Nyerere and President Echeverria of Mexico 'called for the creation of a new international economic order based on equality, justice and co-operation among states. This is the only solution to the serious economic problems facing the world today, particularly the developing nations' (*Daily News*, 29 July 1975).

Look what the governments of the developed countries are doing for their own people. If a certain sector of its population, for instance the farmers, have a living standard below average, the government will subsidise the prices of farm products or restrict imports to guarantee that farmers have a decent income. They pass all kinds of laws to protect the unemployed, the disabled, the under-privileged, the backward people, to ensure them a human existence. The governments do this because they feel responsible for 'their' people. Is it absolutely impossible that something similar is done for the backward nations? Apparently this is not possible, not because it is not good or just to do so, but because Africans, Asians, Latin Americans are not 'their' people, so why bother or care? As long as this national egotism continues, a just world order will remain an idle daydream. Christianity with its care for the under-dog does not stop at the border of one's country.

Development

We all pray for peace, but peace is impossible without justice, as Pope Paul VI said in one of his messages for the Day of Peace: 'If you want peace, work for justice'. But justice is impossible without the development of the third world. So I could add, 'if you want justice, work for development'. If we wish to correct the injustices in the world originating from the extreme inequality among nations, there seems only one solution: promotion of integral development of the under-developed countries. The Church cannot remain passive in this field. True enough, the Church is not *per se* a development agency. But if the Church wishes to remain faithful to the mission she received from Christ, she has to take the side of the poor, the under-privileged, the oppressed, as Christ did in his time. For this reason the Church in Africa has right from the beginning been involved in works of social development. Almost all episcopal conferences have a development department in their secretariats which co-ordinates and stimulates the efforts of the Christians to build their nation. We in Tanzania, for instance, have Caritas Tanzania which functions as the development centre for the Tanzania Episcopal Conference. I am happy to say that Britain, through Mr Noel Charles, Director of CAFOD, has been instrumental in getting Caritas Tanzania organised. Together with the Secretary General of Cor Unum, he visited Tanzania a few years ago to make a pilot study about the possibility of establishing a national co-ordination centre for development. The outcome has been that the already existing Caritas Tanzania has become the instrument of the Episcopal Conference of Tanzania in which the goals of Cor Unum, Caritas Internationalis, Justice and Peace are concentrated. Caritas Tanzania works for development projects sponsored by the Church in co-operation with the government, organises emergency aid in cases of disaster and takes care of the numerous refugees, etc.

We are well aware that in the final analysis the under-developed countries will have to develop themselves, and that they cannot be developed from outside. For this reason we have accepted already for years the policy of self-reliance in Tanzania. As President Nyerere pointed out in the famous *Arusha Declaration*, we can only raise our standard of living by hard work, and not by aid from generous donors. This is a question of principle. But, in fact, the development of our country can be speeded up enormously with development assistance from outside, particularly from the advanced countries.

Task of J&P

The Pontifical Commission for Justice and Peace was asked for by the Vatican Council (*Gaudium et Spes*, n. 90):

In view of the immense hardships which still afflict the majority of men today, the Council regards it as most opportune that some agency be set up for the world-wide promotion of justice for the poor and of Christ's love for them. The role of such agency or organisation will be to stimulate the Catholic community to foster progress in needy regions, and social justice on the international scene.

In *Populorum Progressio* Pope Paul VI described its goals as follows (n. 5):

to bring to the whole of God's people the full knowledge of the part expected of them at the present time, so as to further the progress of poorer peoples, to encourage social justice among nations, to offer to less developed nations the means whereby they can further their own progress.

Be aware

Standing before you, the Commission for International Justice and Peace of the Bishops' Conference of England and Wales, I, a representative of the third world, a son of Africa; what else can I do than plead with you to make the British people aware of the problems of the third world and Africa, to arouse their interest, their sympathy, their will to help to improve our lot? Please, give us a chance. We do not beg for alms and charity. We are willing to stand on our feet, we are willing to develop ourselves, to become self-reliant. But under the present circumstances with the fierce competition of the advanced industrialised nations we simply have not got a chance.

I have pointed out some of our major problems and injustices committed to Africa by the western world, either directly or indirectly:

- continuing colonialism in Rhodesia and Namibia;
- crude racialism in South Africa;
- abuse of internal conflicts by western and eastern powers;
- the use of aid with political strings attached;
- existence of unjust international economic order;
- one-sided trade regulations imposed by industrialised nations;
- nationalism of western countries which makes them indifferent to the problems of the under-developed countries.

All these problems cannot be solved by a group of Christians. They have to be solved by the western nations. I think here we have the first task of the Commission for International Justice and Peace: to arouse the conscience of the people of Britain, their politicians, their government not to close their eyes to what is going on in other parts of the world, and not to worry only about inflation, unemployment, increase of prices. To point out to them the responsibility they have for many of the hardships, oppression, humiliation, exploitation which Africa still undergoes and suffers. We Christians have to be the conscience of the world. And you, members of the Commission for Justice and Peace, have to be the conscience of the British people; not a capitalist conscience, but a Christian conscience.

Partners

A second task should be to establish a partnership between the Church in England and Wales and the churches in the African countries to promote development. This is of a more practical nature, and not entirely new. As I explained above, the episcopal conferences in Africa have their development departments, and are engaged in numerous development projects, relief services, etc. Through your organisations, such as CAFOD, and also through your Commission for Justice and Peace you could channel aid to the development centres of the African episcopal conferences. This type of aid has the advantage over government aid, in that it immediately reaches the people and is usually much more effective and less costly. The projects undertaken by the Church are usually smaller projects, but they have a more immediate impact. Through this contact a fruitful co-operation could emerge between the churches in the developed countries and the churches of the third world. Such co-operation would help to build a bridge between the poor and the rich countries which at present are all too often opposed to each other, and instead of living in harmony and peace, live in open confrontation with each other. As I pointed out in my report on evangelisation at the last Synod (1974): 'Partnership will make the Christian witness more shining in the Catholic Church'.

Governments are hampered by their own nationalism. This nationalism obstructs the effective solution of world problems. But the Church is international by nature and could become a real unifying factor between the nations of the world, by eliminating the factors which bring these nations into conflict with each other.

Change
The fact that you have invited me here to address this conference seems to indicate that you are looking for closer contact and co-operation with the churches of the third world, and Africa in particular. Perhaps some parts of my report may seem to be very critical of the western world. This is certainly not meant as a sign of animosity or of a lack of gratitude for what the Church in England and Wales has done for the third world. It is caused by a sense of

frustration that many western governments are still so reluctant to bring about the fundamental changes in the international order, which can only guarantee lasting peace in the world, based on international justice and on Christian principles. It is caused also by the fear that the slowness of the Christian west to concern itself seriously with the third world will drive many of the third world countries to the communist east.

Before I come to the end of my long talk, let me quote a nice sentence I found in one of the famous *Africa* magazines. It is said that, 'the French boast of being the champions of liberty, the Americans of democracy, and the British of justice' (*Africa*, August 1975). This is indeed a big commendation to the British people. If this is true, then the British people have a challenge. I sincerely wish that my presence here may strengthen your commitment to the cause of international justice and peace.

Bishop Alan Clark (1978)
ECUMENISM – THE GROWING POINT OF UNITY

It is remarkably difficult for anyone immersed in a process, particularly for someone who works largely at the centre, to assess it rightly and therefore to be in a position to say: this is the way ahead, while this other road leads to an unproductive impasse. But, though difficult, it is not impossible – with the obvious proviso that my own judgement is open to question. I have indeed had the great advantage of being at the national centre of ecumenism for almost ten years and have witnessed the growth in Christian unity which has dramatically characterised these years. At the same time I have been engaged, to a limited degree, at the international and European levels. Nevertheless, the movement towards Christian unity, which depends so radically on a real conversion of heart within the Christian churches, touching indeed the basic sources of faith which are the mainspring of their existence as churches, escapes proper definition precisely because it has required so many new categories of thought, so many new attitudes, so many stops and starts. We have been forced to revise many of our presuppositions while, at the same time, holding firm to those doctrines and positions which we see as fundamental to the existence of Christ's Church.

The subject of my lecture this evening must be set against this scenario. I have in mind to isolate the growing points where the goal we are seeking has been significantly advanced. This will involve my identifying to some extent those points where the growth has been retarded or even temporarily suffocated. No one would be so superficial as to suggest either that the growth has been continuous or that the advancement made has been a steady progression. For the process is controlled in its various parts by human contributions or human omissions, and is, therefore, fallible and without inner permanence. Some gains have been lost, and one has had to start again, but, all in all, because the process is the working out in time of a gift of the Holy Spirit, a remarkable picture does emerge of growth in unity. Given greater understanding, greater generosity and therefore greater co-operation, it would be a yet more vivid and inspiring picture. But all those engaged in the work know the wear and tear and drain on human resources that personal involvement implies. So much by way of introduction to the theme.

The first point to be made and emphasised is that now, at this moment, the living experience of the Church is, to a greater or lesser degree, ecumenical. This is, of course, a highly ambiguous statement, and if it were meant to describe what is actually happening within the Christian churches and their congregations, then it is simply false. There is still considerable resistance to the pursuit of Christian unity, particularly when the ecumenical movement threatens the identity of a particular church or community. This is offset, one hopes, by the positive desire endorsed, for example, by recent Catholic pronouncements and documentation, to maintain whole areas in the Christian life and order of particular churches that are peculiar to their tradition, particularly their spiritual heritage. We know the goal is unity in diversity, even if our attempts to explain this or establish the limits of diversity have produced severe tensions and marked differences of approach by the various churches.

However, by the ambiguous statement I have just made, I wish to point to a fact that many still seem unwilling to accept. It is this; it is now inconceivable to promote the mission of a church, which is resolved to renew itself and its spiritual resources, without that church becoming irreversibly involved in the pursuit of Christian unity. I ask you to examine your own experience. By a strange paradox, unless a church accepts this commitment, then it will assuredly relapse into that kind of immobility which contradicts its reason or existence - to be one in order that the world may believe (to use the words of the Lord of the Church) – and makes suspect any claim it may make to catholicity. I am not saying by implication, unite or die. I am saying that such a position of isolation will inevitably lead a church to betray its universal mission, the call to evangelisation at the heart of its vocation. So close is there a connection between reconciliation and renewal that now it is no longer possible to say that the ecumenical movement exists apart from the general life and commitment of the Church. The facts may well be that this is not yet fully accepted: but my first affirmation is that where Christian churches have accepted the necessity for their own renewal, so their commitment to Christian unity, whatever the cost, has deepened – and the reverse is equally true.

This can be put in negative terms as well. It has become increasingly impossible for any church to identify itself over against another Christian church – one of the basic weaknesses in Protestantism. It is not by denying the life and doctrine of our fellow Christians at variance with us that we affirm our identity as the Church of Christ, even when a few of these denials can be substantiated. It is surely for this reason that, while attempting to isolate differences, we are led by the Holy Spirit to affirm the whole series of unities which, to my mind, have held us together as the Body of Christ, however fragile the bonds that have never ceased to exist. The earlier years of the ecumenical movement were marked by the recognition of these unities, and they should be carefully treasured as further advances are contemplated.

The first growing point of unity, therefore, which I would want to emphasise is this spiritual experience and conviction regarding the intimate link between reconciliation in unity and the renewal of the Church and the churches. It is something more than an intellectual conviction. It is an experience which touches the Christian life at its roots – that one has to lose one's life in order to gain it – and this affects us not just as individual Christians but as churches. If this experience is not properly discerned, then we are doomed for ever and a day to degenerate into an assortment of Christian sects in process of dissolution.

I would want, therefore, to draw an important conclusion from this affirmation, namely, that no church can now renew itself independently; it cannot go it alone. The impetus to renew the life of the Church, so strongly felt by so many Christians today and agonised over by an equal number, contains in itself the ecumenical imperative.

I do not doubt that the sceptic will be tempted to say, 'ah! fine aspirations but the facts contradict your picture'. Is this so? The picture is far from being uniform, but the aspiration is more than mere wishful thinking. It may well be that the problems of our contemporary society dictate, to some extent at least, the agenda of the churches and consequently force on the churches the need for a common Christian interpretation. But, wherever the pressure comes from, the desire to speak with one voice is a fact of life, and has long passed mere aspiration. The real problem for the churches is to discern where differences are possible without destroying the unity of the one gospel; at the same time, along with all men and women of wisdom, to acknowledge the new complexities of today's society and to build answers that reflect this awareness. This is the opposite of a plea for ambiguity: it is a strong assertion that the 'newness' of the problems demand patient and honest exploration of their implications for Christian faith.

Recently, the Dean of Peterhouse accused Christian leaders of having adopted the secular culture in which we live and that 'the whole emphasis of contemporary Christianity eschews traditional doctrinal priorities and is about applications'. This criticism has its force. Too much concentration on the earthly city can drag a church away from its primary task of proclaiming a gospel which is not of this world. However, the Church is for the world and is geared to be an effective sign of its salvation. Hence it must be in a position to interpret the *humanum* at its own level and to raise it into the categories of the kingdom of God. If the Dean means to exclude applications of this kind, then I judge this a mistaken road. Mere proclamation of eternal verities lacks credibility, for no human experience is alien to the life and wisdom of the Church of Christ. At the same time we would be unwise not to register assent to the implied criticism that there is a 'doctrinal drift' detectable in some official attitudes to contemporary perplexity.

This is the point, therefore, where I would want to reiterate what has been said so often - that, in the whole process of renewal, precision of doctrine and clarity of teaching are essential. This has been amply verified by the astonishing influence of the agreed statements of the Anglican/Roman Catholic International Commission (ARCIC). For these statements attempt to identify what is specific to faith. Without that identification no renewal of the Church can be long pursued without imminent collapse. At the national level, the work of the Churches Unity Commission has yet to be properly evaluated, but the discernment of faith was at the basis of this unique dialogue. Again, the process of renewal and the process of reconciliation were seen to intersect.

However, of far greater significance for an understanding of the growth in unity at these points of intersection in the official dialogue and structures which link together the Christian Church, is the massive growth of spiritual ecumenism where one is profoundly aware of the heartbeat of renewal. Quite simply, quite astonishingly, there has been, and is, a common experience of the presence of the Holy Spirit in the Church and in the world. This experience has not led Christians away from the Lord but to him, and there has resulted a common adherence to Christ, the one saviour and redeemer of mankind. The experience of 'being brethren' has been of such intensity that it has been and remains extremely difficult to direct and control. But its reality and power cannot be doubted, while its effects on individual Christians are undeniable. But the ecumenist, the one dedicated to the reconciliation of churches as churches, and not as groups of individuals, is entitled to ask: is this experience ecclesial? Does it promote this reconciliation? The answer is, without a shadow of doubt, that it has within it the grace to do so, but not without its being fully integrated into the life - yes, the daily life - of the churches. The rightful appeal to the spirituality of the New Testament requires this integration. Many have seen this; some have not, and therefore put at risk this growth point of unity. These latter, in fact, give the impression of recklessly disregarding the danger signs and are drifting towards another kind of sectarianism. But much doctrinal strength could be given to this spiritual ecumenism if it were openly recognised that what is experienced as a grace of unity at a personal level is in fact the living out of what is, in its interior dynamism, an ecclesial grace. By that I mean, quite simply, that it has within it to make the Church, to further that growth in communion which is directed towards organic unity in all its visible constituent elements.

If the effect of this ecclesial grace is an increasing sense of belonging to the Church, then very humble and careful discernment is required by Church authority and individual Christian alike. There is no impetus in the charismatic grace of renewal - to take one example - for widespread intercommunion. Grave confusion would result from such a persuasion. Without entering that difficult debate, I am content to affirm that more elements of renewal, more external and institutional reconciliation, are demanded before this experience of the Spirit can be embodied, not in intercommunion - the word is an unhappy invention - but in a sacramental communion.

My plea, therefore, is that this grace of renewal, whose source is the Holy Spirit manifesting his work in the Church by a profusion of his gifts, needs to be seen as profoundly ecclesial. A process has been started by what Pope John XXIII regarded as a second Pentecost, and only now has it begun to develop its powerful potential for renewal. It is a vivid growth point of unity - but, like all graces that promote unity, it makes enormous demands on those who are open to it to carry the cross of self-denial and humble themselves before the mighty hand of God in Christ.

It would be logical to continue this paper with an exploration of the many other growth points that you yourselves may wish to see examined and evaluated. But I am convinced that this exercise, however profitable and encouraging, could prove singularly unproductive if we do not stop and ponder again the greatness of the grace of unity as it has been given to the Church. Because we have rightly, and constructively, agreed by and large on the goal of the ecumenical movement (full communion in organic unity), we have been drawn to see in the achieving of the goal the actual gift of God, the grace of unity. I would seriously question this perspective as adequate to what has happened in these last decades. It has, of course, its own logic and within that logic it is valid. But is this the logic of grace? This is my question. For the New Testament always presents the great gifts of the new creation in Christ as both given and not given. We are redeemed once and for all, but we have to work out our redemption in our historic condition within the categories of time and space. We have risen with Christ, and sin and death are now subject to the Lord of all, yet we continue to live in our mortal flesh; we sin, we die. These are only two examples of the mystery of our salvation which can only be perceived by both 'affirming and denying'. My desire is to look at the grace of unity within the same New Testament perspective.

It will, I think, be a better lead-in to the understanding of the grace of unity if I be permitted to make a series of paradoxical and even ambiguous statements. The first is that it is far more important to grow in communion - lower case - than to practise eucharistic sharing. Communion, in this context, is an attempt to translate, however summarily, the rich concept of *koinonia*. At one level, all Christians, by their baptism, enjoy already the *koinonia* of the people of God whereby they are united to the Father, in the Son, by the Holy Spirit. This inner unity is the unmerited grace of the redemption achieved through the death and resurrection of Jesus Christ. But, through estrangement and division, through violent confrontation and hostility, the once visible *koinonia* of the 'undivided Church' was at least partially destroyed – and only in the latter years can it be claimed to have been visibly restored to a greater or lesser degree in the relationship of the Christian churches (hence the tendency to use the term, 'partial communion').

My second affirmation is that this visible *koinonia* is being realised here and now at many levels. Many symbolic acts of church leaders (examples abound) effectively signify the truth of this affirmation. Unless this were so, I cannot see how, even within our self-imposed limits, we could preach the word of God within each other's churches. We could not – again within such limits – share in each other's sacramental life, nor could we, together, share the burden of the Church's mission to the world and be involved in the heavy social problems of contemporary society. But we do – and with good heart. This sharing at a practical level of 'praying and doing together' is the sign of the existence of and a growth in visible communion, the seed-bed of full communion in organic unity.

My third affirmation is more in the nature of a cry that God will save us from what can nullify our ecumenical growth. Central to this growth is the need to resolve those differences that are specific to faith. I have already noticed the destructive force of 'doctrinal drift' – and it is in this area that more effort than ever before is required if we are to grow in catholicity, for we never grow in unity unless we grow in catholicity; we cannot grow in catholicity unless we grow in apostolicity. It is an undeniable experience of those committed to ecumenical dialogue that the patient, demanding dialogue is productive of catholicity of doctrine. But it appears equally true that in living out together the demands of Christian life based on that doctrine, that Christians grow in living communion and increase their catholicity in a dynamic and experiential spirit. For the Roman Catholic, communion must have its visible focal point. It is precisely communion with the See of Rome and its bishop, who sits in 'the chair of unity', that is demanded if the very diversity at the heart of Christian living is to be developed for the benefit of all. It is in this area that, by God's grace and through no human merit, the Roman Catholic Church has shown a heart for renewal unequalled in any other Christian church. From the outside, the problems may seem formidable. At one time they seemed even insoluble to ARCIC, but even the unfinished road constructed by the Commission is a witness to a profound convergence of mind and heart.

Having said that – and, I trust, without ambiguity – let me make my fourth affirmation; the importance now ascribed to the local church (the diocese or district). For the local church is the constituent element of the universal Church; not in the sense that the Church is merely the sum-total of all the local churches, but in the deeply sacramental sense that the universal Church is the communion of all these local churches to the extent that in each the total Church is present in mystery. But this presence is by nature dynamic in the sense that it achieves this realisation of the whole in the part by being in open communion with every local church whose bishop is commissioned to hold us together in unity. Faith admits of a variety of expressions – but it needs to be authenticated by the life and faith of the whole Church.

I am open to the criticism that these four positions which I have sketched in outline do not lead to any firm conclusion about the grace of unity. They certainly do not prove that we have arrived at our goal, that all that is needed is organisational adjustment, that somehow, by some *deus ex machina*, unity will just happen. But I have deliberately introduced these seemingly unrelated ecumenical standpoints in order to win you to a serious consideration of my central contention – that we need, at this historic moment, to look at this grace from a New Testament perspective.

The grace of the ecumenical movement and the grace of unity achieved, the goal of that movement, is one grace, granted by God to his Son in answer to his prayer once and for all, without repentance. To put it more plainly, the grace of unity is already given. I confess, in my foolishness, that this is the only possible explanation of the historic process, visible across the Church of the last twenty-five years. The grace once given has to be worked out, in joy and in pain, through the processes of human history. It is in this sense a continuing race, multiform and complex in its operation, requiring, like all the gifts of God, the freedom of acceptance. The very acceptance is part of the grace. Not only does it require time (the pace has been astonishing), but the more bold its practitioners, the more the discipline of the wisdom of the Spirit is required; the greater the crosses to be borne, the more suffering to be endured; the more soul-searching analysis to be relentlessly pursued, the greater the need to ask for ever-deepening humility.

What I am endeavouring to say, albeit not without stuttering, is that we are now living out the one grace of unity as it has been given to our historic condition. This raises a whole problematic of questions, not least the identification of where that unity substantially resides – but these considerations are not immediately relevant to my quest for understanding. I appeal to the personal experience and reflection of all those devoted to the pursuit of the goal of the movement for Christian unity. I have, clearly, neither the time nor competence to spell out the practical implications of this change of perspective. This will not of itself resolve our continuing disunities in some sort of magical, inanimate way – in fact, the grace of the Spirit so understood makes more stringent demands on faith and charity than ever before. It may well be that it will disclose even greater obstacles to the achievement of the inner dynamism of the once-for-all given grace. God, says the Psalmist, has no time for half-hearted men. The unconvinced or intransigent may well be strengthened in their deeply felt suspicion of the whole enterprise. By our fruits we shall be known - to be right or wrong - and these fruits, if they are given, will be the fruits of the Spirit as he renews the face of the earth.

I ask you to remember that earlier in this paper I defined the goal. The goal remains - and must be laboured for. At this level, nothing has changed. What I have been asking is that we should look at ourselves, as we stand in the grace of God, on the road to the goal. I have unashamedly appealed to experience - the experience of the people of God, the members of Christ's Body, as they meet one another in prayer, in charity and in all manner of good works. I affirm that this experience is more than human fellowship and that it is Spirit-given. But it is given in hope. In the words of Pope Paul VI (addressing the Secretariat of Unity during the Week of Prayer for Christian Unity in 1977):

> *Our hope is founded on God's saving plan. God is almighty and faithful and always fulfils his promise. His word does not return to him without having worked wonders. ... We do not presume to base our hopes on our own works and aspirations, but we boast of our hope in the glory of God. This is the sure word: God in the end will make his glory shine forth and communicate his holiness to all. ... The pouring out of the Holy Spirit into our hearts brings about in Christians a sure transformation, the new man 'until we come to unity in our faith and in our knowledge of the Son of God, until we become the perfect man, fully mature with the fullness of Christ himself' (Ephesians 4:13).*

And then the Holy Father says these words from which I draw enormous comfort and feel that all I have tried to say is not pure foolishness:

> *It is precisely in this perspective that we must set the question for the unity of Christians - growth in faith, maturity in Christ, a tension towards full communion in God. ... Inasmuch as they are baptised, all Christians are individually 'justified by faith and in peace with God through Jesus Christ' (cf. Romans 5:1), but they are also called to draw the full ecclesial consequences from the demands of their common baptism, so that Christ becomes our 'peace', victorious and ecumenical (Ephesians 2:14).*

At this point I hear the words of the Lord to Job, from the heart of the tempest: 'Who is this obscuring my designs with his empty-headed words?' I pray that you will not condemn them too savagely; if my suggestion is wrong, I willingly go back to my ecumenical last if my authorities have not come to the conclusion that it is about time it was taken away from me! Yet I feel that all of you here are very conscious of the pressure of this ecclesial grace, that it is a profoundly disturbing grace, even when it authenticates itself by the peace it brings. We are without options when it comes to articulating the faith we are proud to profess. This we must do. It is not enough to say that there is one faith and many theologies, for some theologies are totally incompatible with that faith. Similarly, we are under the same severe pressure to express in our lives the hope that is in us, exposing that hope to others by the choices we make. Our hope is centred on the kingdom of God and not on the secular city. Our moral standards, however deficient our conduct, must express the life of that kingdom and not be accommodated to the sterile contrivances of a philosophy of man without God. Most of all, we are under the pressure of this ecclesial grace to pursue, without faltering, the ministry of love. These are today's imperatives and in the fulfilment of these we find the growing points.

The consequences? Everything is possible that is not incompatible with the orientation of these pressures - where they are leading us to. Earlier I voiced my conviction that the priority is to develop at all levels the *koinonia* that is at the heart of the grace. Hence, the necessity to use whatever structures are available, wherever they are to be found, that will enable us so to do. This is what living out the grace of ecclesial unity is all about. As that grace is interlocked with the grace of renewal, who would dare to be faint-hearted on the road we have already begun?

In this more than limited paper, I have tried to reflect the '*sensus fidei et ecclesiae*', a genuine '*sensus fidelium*'. It is for you to judge whether I have succeeded.

Bishop Cahal Daly (1979)
NORTHERN IRELAND – FROM IMPASSE TO INITIATIVE

Speaking in London, within the week which has seen, in addition to the killing of a party of soldiers, the lamentable and ignoble killing of Lord Mountbatten of Burma and members of his family in the course of their peaceful family holiday in Donegal, I can only say that Ireland is as stunned and pained and outraged by this deed as the world stands aghast at it. As a Catholic bishop, I wish to avail of this opportunity to express my sincere sympathy to the members of the Royal Family and to the people of Britain in their grief and bewilderment at this terrible deed. Lord Mountbatten was the bearer of a distinguished name, and had added further lustre to that name by his personal service to his country and to humanity. His place in British and in world history is assured. He won the esteem and even the affection of that great people, whose struggle for freedom was once inspired by Ireland's, the people of India, who have decreed seven days of national mourning for his death. It is tragic that such a life should have ended in this brutal way and that Ireland should have been the theatre for such an infamous deed.

It is with real anguish in the soul that one sees the depths to which political violence can descend. A group has claimed to have done this thing in the name of the Irish people. I can only say that the Irish people, in their immense majority, have repudiated and do repudiate, by every means open to them, all such groups and their sinister doings and subversive programmes. Indeed, I must add, that the Irish people are appalled and frightened at the Frankenstein of evil which has been set at large amongst them by the physical force movements. We can scarcely comprehend how men and youths of our own kindred can be brought to the point where such deeds can be calmly planned and coldly done without apparent qualm of conscience.

The essential evil of deeds such as this is that they violate one of the most sacred and fundamental principles of divine commandment and of moral conscience, namely that innocent human life is inviolable, and that any attack upon it is an offence against the majesty of God, whose image is reflected in the human person and whose divine lordship is the guarantor of the sacredness of every human life. In this particular case, there has also been a violation of the sacred laws of hospitality, respect for which has been a proud boast of the Irish people throughout their history from the earliest times. Another cause for sorrow and shame in Ireland is that this deed has been done at a time when the whole Catholic people of Ireland are engaged in intensive spiritual preparation for the pastoral visit of Pope John Paul II. That this time should have been selected for this slaying of the innocent can only fill us with consternation that any group of Irishmen could be so much out of touch with the religious feelings of Irish Catholics at this time, and could bring themselves so to insult and outrage their spiritual sensibilities, as they await, in a spirit of prayerfulness and indeed of 'national spiritual retreat' the coming of their supreme pastor. The nature and the timing of this deed are further evidence, if any were needed, of how foreign to the spirit and the traditions of the Irish people are the philosophy and the ethics and the tactics of those small groups of men who are committed to forcing political change by physical violence. Such philosophies may find mental and moral soul-fellows in the subterranean networks of international terrorism, but they find neither sympathy nor approval nor support among the vast majority of Irish people.

Ten years of sad experience have, however, borne home the lesson that moral denunciation and moral exhortation have very little effect upon people whose minds have been conditioned and whose moral sense has been perverted by the ideology and the ethics of violence. It is more important to try to analyse the factors which have brought this situation about and which serve to perpetuate it, and to examine yet again, but with renewed urgency, proposals which offer reasonable hope that the situations favouring violence might be remedied and the violence itself eventually transcended.

The present paper will argue for four theses in particular:

1. Violence in the north of Ireland has developed such effective strategies for military survival, and has sprouted tentacles clawing into so many departments of social life, that it constitutes a real danger to social and political stability in the whole of Ireland, and a potential threat to democratic institutions in Britain itself. To seek effective policies for ending it is a matter of national interest as well as of historic duty for Great Britain. It is also a matter of national urgency, requiring high priority among Britain's present political concerns.

2. The only effective answer to political violence is to create political institutions providing possibilities for non-violent social change and for peaceful movement towards a more just society.

3. Security policies should be subordinated to and should be at the service of clearly defined and resolutely pursued political aims.

4. The present policy of indefinitely prolonged direct rule is creating a climate conducive to the indefinite prolongation of violence; and it must be replaced urgently by a new political thinking.

The new faces of violence
One can have some degree of sympathy with British spokesmen who might say that they have tried everything in Northern Ireland and can do no more, and that a solution cannot come from them, but must come from the local political representatives. If, however, this thinking were based on the assumption that time is automatically working in the long run on the side of consensus and of peace, or that the situation is anyhow improving as time passes, or that improved security can ultimately bring the violence under

control, or that violence can be eliminated without political settlement, and that, in any case, the basic problem is the violence, and politics must wait until the violence is first eliminated, then I fear that these assumptions will prove to be seriously and dangerously mistaken.

Over the past ten years, and at an accelerating rhythm since the breakdown of Sunningdale and the fall of the Executive in 1974, the situation in Northern Ireland has deteriorated with every year that passed. The republican militarists have not only acquired new sophistication in methods and tactics of guerrilla warfare. They have not only arrived at a high degree of efficiency in their techniques of survival. They have not only become more coldly efficient and ruthless in their definition and pursuit of 'targets'. They have also mastered the grammar of international terrorism and immersed themselves in its cluster of fanatical ideologies. They have developed sinister links with international terrorist organisations, and can rival many of these in sophistication and 'professionalism'. We are not confronted any longer with amateur, much less with armchair revolutionaries, but with experienced and resourceful professionals. They boast of their new professionalism, though killing is a profession to which few would take pride in belonging.

The cadres of the activist republican groups have also become adept in the techniques of infiltrating many apparently neutral sectors of community life. They have built up complex networks of business interests. Despite a professed ideological detestation of capitalism, they have extended tentacles into trade and commerce, the property market, housing allocation, the illegal drink trade, transport operations. Some obscurity still surrounds a recent find in the Republic of a huge drug-smuggling operation, but that this should be shown to have links with subversive groups would be completely in character with their other known activities. All this is in addition to the various forms of 'protection racket' which have been a long-standing feature of IRA, UDA and UVF groups in the north of Ireland. Such activities, apart from being a very lucrative source of funds for the subversive organisations, also enable them to burrow deep into the fabric of communities. Its systematic infiltration into so many of the patterns of community relationships makes subversive violence very difficult to eradicate from a community into which it has pushed its roots. Such activities make it hard to demarcate subversive crime from non-political crime, and make the detection and elimination of either form of crime immensely difficult. It is impossible to say, for example, how much of the epidemic of bank raids, which we have had over recent years in both parts of Ireland, is traceable to 'ordinary' criminals, and how much to subversives, or indeed how much might be due to a sinister compact between the two.

It could easily be foretold, many years ago, that subversive violence could not long be contained within the territory of Northern Ireland. It was both geographically unavoidable and politically predictable that it would 'spill over' into the Republic. This has happened to a disturbing degree. The republican movements are as much committed to the subversion of the democratic institutions of the Republic of Ireland as they are to the institutions of what they choose to call 'British rule' in Northern Ireland. Their language regarding the political institutions of what, in common with loyalist bigots, they call 'the Free State', is as vitriolic as that which they use about British institutions. At the present time, counter-subversive security measures are costing the citizens of the Republic of Ireland proportionately more *per capita* than even the enormous cost to British tax-payers of security in Northern Ireland. This, by the way, is an interesting commentary on the claim, of which sometimes one still hears echoes, that the Republic of Ireland has no business 'interfering in the affairs of the United Kingdom'. Neither the United Kingdom, with its immense commitment of men and resources to Northern Ireland security, nor the Republic, with its relatively massive security commitments, can claim great success in counter-terrorist operations. This should temper accusations of security failure in the Republic.

The longer this situation continues, the greater the risk to peace and order in the Republic of Ireland, if not, indeed, in these islands as a whole. I fear that the long drawn-out continuance of political violence in this island, if conjoined with economic difficulties, unemployment, particularly youth unemployment, and inflation, in the Republic, could constitute a combination which would be full of danger to social and political stability and to democratic institutions all over Ireland. The Irish bishops, in the pastoral letter on justice in 1977, warned about the 'very great dangers of grave social and socio-political tension', which could ensue from failure to face the challenges of unemployment and social justice in the present situation in Ireland.

It is, therefore, time that politicians in Britain gave up any illusion that the Northern Ireland problem can safely be left to 'sort itself out', or that it can safely be postponed until urgent domestic problems regarding the economy, etc., can be solved.

A religious conflict?

Several recent commentators on the treatment of the Northern Ireland conflict in the British media have deplored the absence of analysis of the situation, and the facile recourse to such simplistic formulae as that of 'religious war'. This is, at most, a half-truth, which can be convenient to politicians in the short term, but which can be highly dangerous in the long run, as diverting attention from the political aspects of the conflict. I would argue that the use of the terms 'Protestant' and 'Catholic' to describe the parties in conflict has become so unhelpful as to be positively an obstacle to objective analysis and to the search for a solution.

The use of religious terms obscures the issue. These terms describe sociological groups which historically have had, and which continue to have, many distinct and even opposing features. One of these is indeed religious denomination. But there are many others, including economic, social, cultural and political features. The cultural, socio-economic and political features have much more relevance to the present conflict than has the denominational affiliation. Solutions to the conflict must be sought in these areas. The relevance of the strictly religious factor is marginal, rather than central. The effect upon the violence of strictly religious activity, in the sense of ecumenical dialogue and efforts towards denominational reconciliation, is limited. Such activities are good and necessary in themselves. They are an imperious Christian duty for all the churches. But they neither have nor can have a decisive impact on the actual violence. What the churches can do to 'solve' the problems of violence is extremely circumscribed. Indeed, it has been humbling for Irish churchmen over the past ten years to be brought face to face with their relative powerlessness in situations of armed conflict.

One consequence of seeing the Northern Ireland problem in religious terms has been the appeal to such remedies as that of 'integrated schooling'. I do not propose to discuss that complex issue here. I merely wish to refer to some conclusions of James Russell, who has to his credit an impressive body of research into this whole question. He recounts that he came to Northern Ireland in the 1960s sharing 'the popular assumption that separate schooling for Protestants and Catholics leads to, or at least reinforces, discord, disorder and consequent violence'. He expected research to confirm this assumption. Instead, his research convinced him that this hypothesis is at variance with the facts. He concluded that it even distracts attention from the real causes of discord and the real directions along which solutions must be sought. He declares:

It is unrealistic to expect schools to create attitudes in pupils which are conducive to common allegiance in Northern Ireland, in the absence of support from the adult community and the existence of a political institution which is generally accepted as fair and impartial. … Only when there is some fundamental agreement on a political structure for Northern Ireland, can we expect the main general agents of socialisation to provide experiences that will gradually combine to determine how an individual will play his role as a citizen.

It is my conviction (and here I do not attribute these views to Russell) that resentments in the minority community derive from its permanent, unchanging and apparently unchangeable experience of being excluded from the decision-making processes of government. This inevitably fosters a sense of alienation, of not belonging, of being 'against the government', 'against the establishment', an 'establishment' which has always been, and seems always intended to continue to be, 'them' and never 'us'. One does not have to be a social psychologist to realise that this experience creates very serious obstacles to the development of a sense of identification with the institutions and organs and agencies of government. This is basically a political problem, for which political solutions have to be sought. In other words, and here I again quote James Russell, political institutions must be sought which would 'accept the differences in aspiration and religion on a separate-but-equal basis and try to regulate the conflict'.

John White has studied several nineteenth century situations of apparently 'sectarian' conflict, which have analogies to the Northern Ireland situation. He finds these situations in various British cities, as well as in urban areas in the United States, in Germany and in Austria. In each of these cases, there was an economic and social and political aspect as well as a religious aspect to the conflict. A Protestant workforce, or, as the case might be, a Catholic ascendancy, felt threatened in its economic or employment security or in its political stability by a religious minority. In every single case, however, as White shows, the sectarian conflict was resolved; resolved, however, not by theological discussion and not by ecumenical activity, but rather by political development and socio-economic progress. The solution in every case came from movement towards a political situation in which the denominational minority could participate in the political process, and thereby acquire both some degree of political power and a sense of political responsibility.

I believe that this analysis is extremely relevant to the Northern Ireland situation. The struggle in Northern Ireland is about power, not about theology or worship. It is about civic and political rights, about freedom and equality of political allegiance and cultural expression. It is about wealth and its distribution, about privilege, about equality of opportunity. It is about jobs, and prospects of employment and promotion. It is about location of industry, and deployment of resources. It is about who controls what and who shares what and who has access to what; and about who can take the decisions which determine all these questions. These are all questions of politics; they are questions of justice.

Politics and justice

Churchmen have their responsibilities. We must not attempt to deny them. I hope we will not shirk them. But churchmen cannot deliver solutions to the questions I have been discussing, and these questions are basic to the whole Northern Ireland problem. Political questions must be given political solutions.

Any objective analysis of the Northern Ireland situation must begin by recognising that there exist two historic communities in Northern Ireland, which are differentiated by their diverse understandings of history, their contrasting experiences of access to power and privilege and opportunity. These are not matters of abstract theorising. They have had very positive results, in the contrasting socio-economic profile of both communities, in terms of job prospect, average size of income, distribution of income groups over the population - as the figures from the recent report from the Fair Employment Commission placed beyond argument.

In the concrete Northern Ireland situation, I am convinced that justice as between the two historic communities requires that representatives of the minority community be given proportionate but real access to the levels where the political decisions are taken which determine the distribution of power and wealth and opportunity, the allocation of industries, resources and jobs. It is a matter for political discussion and negotiation how this can be brought about. Whatever means are adopted, there will be no inherent reason requiring that this arrangement be permanent. But only some effective machinery of this kind will create a possibility for political movement. There can be no escape for either community from the vicious spiral of violence.

John White has argued that the alleviation of sectarian conflict in other countries has come about only when 'one or other group of politicians found it in their interest to build a coalition cutting across denominational boundaries'. There can be no beginning of movement in that direction until, to start with, representatives of the minority community have real prospect of participation in real political power. I repeat that the ways in which this sharing of political power can be brought about are political questions in which, as a churchman, I have no competence. But I must say firmly as a bishop that I believe this sharing of access to political power is itself a matter of justice transcending politics.

If anyone doubts this, let him think seriously about the effects on a whole community of its being regarded as unfit to be trusted to exercise power responsibly, as incapable of sharing effectively and responsibly in the government of its homeland. Surely this constitutes a manifest affront to human dignity, a clear denial of political justice.

A relevant British analysis

There exists, in fact, an official analysis of the conflict in Northern Ireland, emanating from the British government itself, which concurs with several of the points which I have tried to make above. I refer to the Green Paper, *The Future of Northern Ireland*, of October 1972. This I believe to be one of the most penetrating analyses of the Irish problem ever to issue from an official British source. This document recognised that the essence of the Northern Ireland problem is that there are two communities in Northern Ireland, whose radically different historical, political, and indeed national traditions excluded the very consensus on fundamental political issues which are the normal and the necessary presupposition of a democratic state. The document states: 'The special feature of the Northern Ireland situation was that the great divide in political life was not between different viewpoints on such matters as the allocation of resources and the determination of priorities, but between two whole communities.' This analysis led the then British government to the conclusion that:

The two primary purposes of any new institutions must be first to seek a much wider consensus than has hitherto existed, and second to be such as will work efficiently and will be capable of providing the concrete results of good government: peace and order, physical development, social and economic progress. This is fundamental because Northern Ireland's problems flow not just from a clash of national aspirations or from friction between the communities, but also from social and economic conditions such as inadequate housing and unemployment. ...

A Northern Ireland assembly or authority must be capable of involving all its members constructively in ways which satisfy them and those they represent that the whole community has a part to play in the government of the province. As a minimum this would involve assuring minority groups of an effective voice and a real influence; but there are strong arguments that the objective of real participation should be achieved by giving minority interests a share in the exercise of executive power. ...

There must be an assurance, built into any new structures, that there will be absolute fairness and equality of opportunity for all. The future administration of Northern Ireland must be seen to be completely even-handed both in law and in fact.

Everything that has happened since has demonstrated beyond any possibility of doubt that it is only along lines such as these that any acceptable solution, with any hope of laying foundations for lasting peace, can be based. In a situation in which there are, within the same territory, two communities, with two radically different conceptions of what would be a viable solution, there must obviously be an ultimate arbitrator or guarantor whose decisions and limiting conditions must be final. In any case, the Northern Ireland territory has never been nor seen itself as being an autonomous entity with a sovereign parliament. It cannot and should not be expected to take sovereign decisions.

Furthermore, each community has traditionally looked beyond itself for the source of its identity and the goal of its aspirations. One community has as its most cherished heritage a British dimension; the other has as its most characteristic identification an Irish dimension. For either of the two governments envisaged in these dimensions to say that it is 'a problem for the people of Northern Ireland to solve for themselves', would be an abdication of responsibility and a refusal to recognise the realities of the problem. There is a British dimension and an Irish dimension in Ulster politics, and they can neither of them be dismissed as importations from outside, or as alien to the situation and able to be eliminated from its solution. An Irish dimension, just as much as a British one, is an internal dimension of the Ulster political problem, and any viable solution must give recognition to it. Equally, there is a Northern Ireland dimension in Irish politics, and it also is an internal not an external problem.

Finally, the Irish problem is a problem of domestic politics for Britain, and it deserves and needs the commitment of the best political brains which Britain has at her disposal at the present time. It is Britain which, in the last analysis, must determine the parameters of a solution, and must, with impartial justice and at the same time with firmness and finality, convince both communities that these ultimate parameters are the conditions governing further elections and consultations. Statesmen have, after all, a duty to lead and not only to consult. There are situations in which a community may not even know 'the things which are for its peace', and it is the duty of those who bear the ultimate responsibility for peace to confront them with the realities of 'the time of their visitation'.

The term, 'power sharing', may have become emotive as much as descriptive. Its descriptive content may have become distorted or diluted by over-use. But the reality behind the term retains all its relevance in the search for a political solution. Both major parties in Britain have so far retained and frequently reaffirmed their commitment to some form of real sharing of power between the communities in Northern Ireland. I trust that politicians and the general public in Britain realise the extreme gravity of the implication of any suggestion of an abandonment of that commitment, whether overtly or by a device which would retain the words, but evacuate the content. The disastrous situation in Northern Ireland calls urgently for new movement towards a political settlement embodying political justice and equality of rights with accompanying equality of responsibilities for both communities.

Meanwhile, there is, alas, the terrible reality of the continuing violence. An ill-conceived phrase was once put into circulation, that of 'an acceptable level of violence'. There is no such thing as an 'acceptable level' of murders. There is no acceptable level of such crimes as that committed last Monday in a holiday boat off the Irish coast at Mullaghmore. Security is an inescapable necessity. The present week is not a propitious time to make the case that certain security policies not only do not maintain or reduce the violence, but actually serve to fuel it. Of this, however, I am profoundly convinced; and it is my very abhorrence of violence which constrains me to question several aspects of security policies in Northern Ireland.

Security policies

The Northern Ireland problem is much more than a security problem, and security successes alone will never solve the problem. The elimination of violence would indeed be a mighty achievement, bringing unqualified relief to both Northern Ireland communities. But, even if the present violence were completely eliminated, Northern Ireland would remain a chronically politically unstable and violence-prone society, unless the root causes of the violence were firmly tackled, and unless the political structures of a just society, recognised and accepted as such by the majority of people in both communities, were established. Those concerned about peace in Ireland should be vigilant about any presentation of the problem as merely a security problem, or one susceptible of military settlement.

Secondly, security decisions and policies should be open to review and should never be given the status of inflexible principle. Moral detestation of and just retribution for proven crimes are one thing – and there is unquestionable need for both in Northern Ireland, where crimes have been horrible and guilt has been undeniable, and has often been fully proven – but those who determine security policies must be concerned also about their practical effectiveness in achieving their aim, namely the elimination of violence. If it were found that, on the contrary, certain security policies merely extend the range of alienation and resentment, if it were found that certain policies merely increase the flow of recruits into subversive organisations, if it were found that certain security policies merely created conditions for the deeper and longer indoctrination of prisoners into the ideology and methodology of subversion, then surely the policies in question should be suspected to be counter-productive and should be reviewed. Security policies can serve merely to recycle violence, rather than to eliminate it.

I believe that there have been mistakes and excesses in security policies, and that many of these can be traced to the conviction that the Northern Ireland problem is primarily a security problem, to be solved by security measures. A recent sociological study of 'struggles in a Belfast community' by Frank Burton, entitled *The Politics of Legitimacy*, remarks:

> *The threat that national and international political violence poses, both to governments and to potential victims, has generated a widespread concern with the nature of political violence. Most of this concern ... has taken the form of an interest in counter-insurgency techniques. The practical interest in combating 'terrorism' has relegated the explanation of its origin and forms to a secondary position. Indeed, the very attempt to explain the incidence of any particular form of political violence is liable to be branded by, for example, counter-insurgents as the propaganda of sympathisers. Politicised violence is, however, too important a social phenomenon to be left to the theorists of social control.*

It should surely be possible, after ten years, to have devised security policies which would be as little oppressive as possible to peaceful and law-abiding people in their streets and in their homes, and would be less likely to alienate people who have neither association nor sympathy with terrorists. It should be possible to avoid or to extricate oneself from policies which are easily exploited by terrorists for their propaganda purposes.

The third thing I wish to say in this connection is that security policies and practices, like all human affairs, are subject to the moral law of respect for human rights and human dignity. This sounds a platitude, but it can be overlooked, because we all grant presumptions in favour of our own army and police forces, and the institutions and processes which they serve. These presumptions are often justified. But they are not automatically just. It takes a deliberate effort from all of us to surmount the 'idols of our tribe' and to be objective about the 'sacred cows' of our nation.

The subject of torture or degrading treatment is emotionally explosive where the security forces of our own country are concerned. We must, however, try to triumph over emotion by moral reason and conscience. On this question, I shall only say that a dispassionate reading of the Compton, Gardiner and Bennett reports shows that abuses did exist, that abuses are always possible, and that moral vigilance over security policies is necessary. Counter-insurgency is not an absolute beyond the moral law. It is always so much more easy to recognise security excesses in far-off lands than to recognise them in our own. But the Christian cannot evade the duty of moral vigilance, or forget the Lord's injunction about the visual block in one's own eye.

The political vacuum

The present Northern Ireland regime of 'direct rule' from Westminster was first introduced as a short-term and strictly interim provision, which was intended to create the context for rapid movement towards new political structures. It was not originally intended to be in itself a political answer to Northern Ireland's problems. Its indefinite prolongation, in the absence of any political policy, has proved to have consequences quite contradictory of the original intention. Direct rule has become an obstacle to movement towards a political solution. To have allowed the policy of the Green Paper of 1972, and the ensuing constitutional proposals of 1973, to fall into ruin, and to have done nothing since to rebuild on the ruins, is a serious abdication of political responsibility. The political vacuum which exists in Northern Ireland today is unpardonable, and it is disastrous. If revolutionaries be fish that need suitable water in which to swim, then that water at this time is not so much sympathy in the ghettos as the messy mix of direct rule, security methods without apparent political policy, and total lack of political initiative.

Direct rule means the suspension of local politics, the absence of seriousness in local discussion of politics, the lack of any credible political alternative to the violence. When there is no official forum for political debate, parties fragment, the best lose interest and opt out, the worst intrigue and obstruct with passionate intensity. Politicians are off-staged by paramilitaries; politics becomes discredited; all initiative is given over to men of violence. Security measures alienate the innocent and leave them open to exploitation by the paramilitaries. The absence of political initiative on the part of the administration combines with other elements to generate in people a sense of hopelessness. It is even more true towards the end of 1979 than it was when the northern Catholic bishops first said it in 1971: 'Far-reaching political initiatives must be sought as a matter of great urgency if those who advocate violence are to be deprived of their chief ally - despair.'

There must now be movement beyond and out of the present impasse. I shall quote again from the government Green Paper:

It can be argued that the British democratic system only works where a regular alternation of parties is possible; that the real test of a democratic system is its ability to provide peaceful and orderly government and that by that standard the existing system has failed in Northern Ireland; that other countries with divided communities have made their special constitutional provision to ensure participation by all; that a number of these countries have had stable and successful coalition governments over many years; and that there is no hope of binding the minority to the support of new political arrangements in Northern Ireland unless they are admitted to active participation in any new structures.

The British government itself solemnly warned in 1974 that, if its constitutional proposals were rejected or frustrated, disaster would follow. It declared:

They can be frustrated if interests in Northern Ireland refuse to allow them to be tried, or if any one of the communities is determined to impose its will on another. It should now be perfectly clear that these are prescriptions for disaster. The government believes, however, that the majority of the people of Northern Ireland have an overwhelming desire for peace and that they will accept the opportunity which these proposals offer.

The fruits of peace

It is an under-statement to say that the restoration of peace and stability in Northern Ireland will not be easy or rapid. A will to co-operate between all those concerned in the complex tragedy is required. The Northern Ireland political parties, the government and the opposition in Britain, the government and the opposition in the Republic, all have their part to play, their obligations to accept. I speak only of the political agents. I am not forgetting the churches. We too have our distinct but inescapable obligations, and we shall not shirk them.

The difficulties are immense, but the fruits of success are incalculable. It would indeed be rash to under-estimate the risks for all of us in these islands of not finding solutions for the Northern Ireland problem. But, on the other hand, it would be difficult to exaggerate the benefits for all of us which would flow from bringing about a peaceful and just and reconciled society in Northern Ireland.

If Britain were to set herself with enlightenment, determination and courage to find a solution to the Irish problem, the goodwill generated thereby in her neighbouring island and among the Irish diaspora all over the world would be a political asset of very considerable importance, and would enhance Britain's credibility and influence as a force for peace and reconciliation and justice in the world. The exemplary significance for Europe and for the world of the settlement of a problem so deeply rooted in history as the Irish problem, would be of historic significance and would be of considerable international political importance.

The history of Anglo-Irish relations has not always been a happy one. One consoling fact emerges, however, from that history; namely that, when relations between our two peoples are established on a basis of equality of rights, of dignity and of reciprocal respect, then a spontaneous friendship and even affinity between our two peoples asserts itself. The British politician who shall have set himself the task of achieving peace in Northern Ireland, and thereby permanent peace and friendship between our two islands, would have an honoured place in history. To work for this, on both sides of the Irish channel, could be our most appropriate joint monument to the memory of the late Lord Mountbatten of Burma.

Reconciliation

I shall end by one word to myself and to my brother-churchmen. We are prone to preachers' words and preachers' attitudes. We easily appear as sentimentalists, romantics, other-worldlings, abounding in a rhetoric remote from reality and using words which disguise the all-too-human stuff of men and of society.

We preach reconciliation; but we seem often to mean by it that some words are to be spoken, some gestures are to be performed, but that nothing actually has to be changed, no one actually has to change. But reconciliation is not verbal formulae or ritual gestures. Reconciliation is change; its meaning is in the changes that actually happen. Reconciliation in Northern Ireland will begin to happen, not when Protestant and Catholic churchmen walk arm in arm down our Royal Avenue in Belfast; but when structures of political partnership are functioning, when barriers to opportunity are removed on both sides, when avenues of employment are open to all, when disparities of wealth and privilege between communities are reduced, when human dignity is accorded equal rights and equal respect, regardless of address or school or church or chapel. The gestures can happen then, because only then will they be sincere. Before that has happened, they might be only clerical games.

What I am saying is not some social horizontalism substituted for the gospel of Jesus Christ. What I am saying is basic Christianity. It is gospel truth. I have been merely spelling out the meaning of conversion, of *metanoia*. Men have to change, change themselves radically, before their repentance is real. The test whether they have changed is to be found in what they do, more than in what they say. It is to be found in the structures of their society more than in their feelings of generalised benevolence.

We have a command of the Lord to establish reconciled structures and exercise reconciled behaviour, rather than merely cultivate feelings of reconciliation. This is made by the Lord a test of faith itself, when he says, 'Repent and believe the gospel'. This is how we have to 'redeem the time' before he comes again, for he comes quickly (*Revelation* 22:20).

Cardinal Johannes Willebrands (1985)
IS CHRISTIANITY ANTI-SEMITIC?

It is a pleasure and an honour for me, as President of the Holy See Commission for Religious Relations with the Jews, to lecture at this Oxford Union, at the same podium where many illustrious personalities have already spoken. Let me express the hope at the outset, that in this year, during which we celebrate the twentieth anniversary of the promulgation of the conciliar declaration *Nostra Aetate* on the relations between the Church and the non-Christian religions, that my talk may help to improve still more the relations between the Church and the Jewish people, and also eventually to dispel certain stereotypes sometimes heard about the Church and her teaching on Judaism.

The subject I have been asked to speak on is expressed in the question: is Christianity anti-Semitic? Before I enter into the substance of the answer I intend to give to this question, I believe we must pause for a moment to examine carefully the terms of the question. Is Christianity anti-Semitic? One could ask, to begin with, what does the word 'Christianity' mean in this context? Does it mean a body of belief and practice or, as the time honoured Latin expression goes, *fides et mores*? Does it mean, instead, a certain cultural world, more or less inspired by such belief and practices? Does it mean a group of men and women, in a certain moment of history, who are held to be somehow linked to the Christian faith? These three meanings, while connected among themselves, do not exactly overlap.

In the same way it could also be asked, what does 'anti-Semitic' mean in the question above? Is it the original 'racist' sense, intended by W Marr, who first coined the term in 1879? Or is it meant in a broader sense, including prejudices and stereotypes against Jews and

Judaism, more or less religiously inspired? Or is it a yet broader sense, with political overtones?

In the face of all this, I am convinced that to answer in a straightforward way the question in the title of this lecture, some ambiguities ought first to be dispelled. In order to do this in an orderly fashion I shall proceed step by step. First, however, I shall propose a kind of thesis: namely, if 'Christianity' is taken to mean the distinctive body of Christian faith and practice, as professed and lived out, albeit imperfectly, in the Christian churches, it cannot be said that Christianity is 'anti-Semitic'. But I must immediately add that 'anti-Semitic', in the last sentence of this thesis, should be understood in the first and in the second sense spelled out above, without political overtones. Let me now try to prove, or illustrate, this thesis.

Is the New Testament anti-Semitic?

As the normative text for Christianity is the Bible, as the Word of God, and particularly (but not exclusively) the New Testament part of the Bible, I would like to start by considering this question: is the New Testament anti-Semitic? As you are well aware, this question has been answered in the affirmative, and it is only honest to say, more by Christian than by Jewish scholars.

Regarding this question, the following points should be carefully weighed. Firstly, the New Testament contains a series of pro-Semitic statements, which I would like quickly to refer to here, without in any way listing them all:

- 'Salvation is from the Jews' (*John* 4:22).
- Paul twice goes out of his way to profess his attachment to Judaism. In *Romans* 9:1-5, of which I shall only quote verbatim this verse: 'Indeed, I could even wish to be separated from Christ (*anathema*, in the Greek text) for the sake of my brothers, my kinsmen, the Israelites'. And in *Philippians* 3:4-6: 'I was

circumcised on the eighth day, being of the stock of Israel, a Hebrew of Hebrew origin'.

• And, last but not least, Luke's (a Gentile!) remarkably positive presentation of the Jewish way of worship and/or the Jewish way of life, in his narrative of the infancy of Christ (2:21-38) and in his narrative of the nascent Church (*Acts* 3:1; 5:41-42). Are not both these careful descriptions, parallel one to the other, a way of affirming the Jewish matrix of the Lord and his Church, however artful Luke's literary construction may be thought to be?

Secondly, at a still deeper level, the writers of the New Testament quite consciously place Jesus and his mission in the continuation of the Old Testament and the contemporary Jewish tradition. Before I get to the specific points following hereafter, I would like to stress this last reference to the 'Jewish tradition'. It should be borne in mind, that between the last books of the Old Testament in Hebrew and Aramaic or Greek, and the first written texts of the New Testament, there is a whole period, called for this reason 'intertestamental', with a rich and varied literature and with oral traditions, some of which have been revealed to us by the so-called Dead Sea Scrolls and other recent manuscript discoveries. This variegated body, or rather bodies, of Jewish religious and cultural expression, should be considered carefully when the relationship between the second and the first Testaments is assessed. Between one and the other, or more concretely between the last Old Testament writings and Jesus, stands all this multiple oral and literary material, which sometimes helps to explain what in the Jewish background of the New Testament does not find a clear enough explanation in the Old Testament.

I shall also list here - as I did above - some texts or themes, without at all trying to be exhaustive:

• Jesus' Jewish origins and attachments are revealed, not dissimulated, even to the Gentiles, who knew, most of them at least, next to nothing about Judaism. Texts to be highlighted in this connection are: *Romans* 1:14 ('the Son of God, descended from David according to the flesh'); *Galatians* 4:4 ('God sent forth his son ... born under the law'). *Luke* chapters 1 and 2, already mentioned, belong here too. Thus the most ancient kerygmatic presentation of Jesus, son of man and son of God, included an explicit reference to his Jewishness.

• Jesus' mission was directed in the first place to Israel. The Gospel writers are very much aware of this and even make an explicit formulation of this point when it is a question of opening up that mission to the Gentiles. See *Matthew* 15:24 in the story of the Canaanite woman: 'My mission is only to the lost sheep of the house of Israel'. The apostles, also in their first mission, are enjoined to do exactly the same: 'Do not visit pagan territory and do not enter a Samaritan town. Go instead after the lost sheep of the house of Israel' (*Matthew* 10:5-6).

This order of mission was scrupulously kept by the apostles after the resurrection, as it is easy to see in the book of *Acts*, where Paul always starts his apostolic visits in the local synagogue (eg. 13:5), but also in the programmatic assertion of the same Paul in *Romans* 1:17: '(the gospel) is the power of God leading ... to salvation, the Jew first, then the Greek'. It could be said, quite truly, that this preference or priority (if not exclusiveness, in Jesus' own mission), is expressed later on by Paul in his well-known parable of the wild olive branches grafted on to the good olive tree (*Romans* 11:12). In this same connection, one should point to all such texts where the New Testament writers find the confirmation – or, if you wish, the foundation – of Jesus' identity and mission, in the 'law, the prophets and the psalms' (*Luke* 24:44). This is why the universal Church, as articulated by Irenaeus in the east and Tertullian in the west, so decidedly and unhesitatingly rejected Marcionism (which dismissed the Old Testament and taught that Christ was the son of a good, non-

Jewish god). If one tries to cut off the New Testament from the Old it will soon be obvious that the New Testament goes asunder too. Thus Paul found it quite natural to affirm, in *Romans* 3:31: 'Are we then abolishing the law by means of faith? Not at all! On the contrary, we are confirming the law as the law confirms Christ.'

Thirdly, it would be rather easy to extend the former section to the main concepts, imagery and language of the New Testament. They come first and foremost from the Old Testament. There was a time in biblical scholarship when the trend was to read and interpret the New Testament writings in the light of Greek or rather late Hellenic culture and religion. This trend has not entirely died out. But I think it is only fair to say that what is seen and appreciated now by scholars is the deep, essential Jewish character of the New Testament. To illustrate briefly this change of orientation, I shall mention just two items: the interpretation of the book of *Revelation* in the light of biblical apocalyptic imagery, taken, almost intact, from *Isaiah* (chapter 6), *Ezekiel* (1:10), and *Daniel* (*passim*), with besides a real influx from Jewish apocalyptic writings; messianic titles, however reinterpreted and given a new meaning, in the New Testament, all come from the Old Testament, or the Hebrew Bible, while a title like 'son of man', notwithstanding the many problems connected with it, has some kind of relation to the same title in contemporary Jewish apocalyptic literature (the book of *Enoch*).

At this point we could perhaps draw a first, provisional, conclusion: to affirm that the New Testament is anti-Semitic would be tantamount to affirming that it is, in itself, contradictory. In fact, it is not at all easy to find a book more Semitic or more Jewish than the New Testament. To try to tear off from the New Testament its Semitic substance, would simply mean to destroy it, lock, stock and barrel. I recall here again Marcion's self-defeating enterprise and the Church's reaction against it. Now, Christianity, in the first sense indicated above, embodies the New Testament.

Anti-Semitism in the New Testament

But let us make another, more difficult step: does the New Testament contain anti-Semitic statements? No doubt, while affirming with utmost energy, as I just did, the Jewishness of Jesus and of the writings witnessing to him, I must, in all honesty, face the objections which might spring from the texts of those same books, and see if they would make us change my thesis. Let me consider some of them at least, first by listing them, next by trying to deal with the challenge they present.

Firstly, there are in the New Testament some affirmations which, at first sight, seem, at the very least, critical of and negative towards the Jews, such as *1 Thessalonians* 2:14-16 ('they displease God and oppose everyone') and *Matthew* 27:25 ('let his blood be on us and on our children').

Secondly, some texts, if not complete books, of the New Testament present 'the Jews' in an unfavourable light. The case in point, as is known to all, is the Gospel of *John*, where 'the Jews' appear mostly (but not always) as the opposers of Jesus' person and mission, entirely closed to both and indeed because of an obvious lack of good will (or 'blindness', as in the story of the man born blind in chapter 9, which could be taken as paradigmatic).

Thirdly, the Pharisees are frequently (but again not always) pictured as forming a very negative, hypocritical, falsely religious group, a presentation which, unfortunately, has contributed to giving to that name, in many languages, a decisively derogatory ring - quite unjustly, in the opinion of many, not only Jews but also Christians.

What could, or should, be said of such texts and pictures, to which more could be added? In fact, it must be admitted that texts such as these have had a long lasting negative effect on the Christian view of Jews and Judaism. In fact, it must also be admitted that they have had anti-Semitic consequences. Still, if we are to keep to the terms of the question which gives its title to this lecture, it cannot be said, because of this, that either the New Testament or Christianity as such (in the sense explained above) are anti-Semitic. These texts and descriptions do not, in any way, cancel or modify the other, positive thrust of the New Testament regarding matters Jewish. It is true that they are there, and have to be explained (not explained away), but they do not put into question the fundamental Jewishness, not only of Jesus, but of the New Testament as such, Paul included. Indeed, it is in light of this basic Jewishness that such texts should be read and interpreted, and certainly not the other way around.

It is here perhaps that a certain Christian tradition may be found to be defective. For centuries an image of Jews and Judaism has been projected which was inspired mostly, if not exclusively, by such negative references. The positive thrust was never forgotten (as I shall point out later on), but it certainly did not play any dominant role. In this sense, what we are trying to do now, after the declaration *Nostra Aetate* (n. 4), and the 1974 *Guidelines and Suggestions* for its implementation, is to link with that truer, normative past, always living in the New Testament.

After having said this, I now turn to the problematic texts and descriptions I have referred to. Firstly, if 'the Jéws' are criticised, I am not aware of any radical condemnation, or even criticism, of Judaism, as it was known and practised at that time. Even Paul's severe critique of the law presupposes always that the law is 'good' in itself, which he says explicitly at least twice (*Romans* 7:12; *1 Timothy* 1:8). The epistle to the Hebrews speaks mostly about what we have called later the 'ceremonial' law and that aspect of the Mosaic covenant (not the Abrahamic one) which deals with worship (*Hebrews* 8:13). This is why it was not held to be contradictory, much less 'un-Christian', to participate in the temple worship and ceremonies, even after the resurrection, let alone before (*Acts* 3:1; *John* 10:21 and *passim*), even by Paul himself (*Acts* 21:26). This, of course, ended with the complete separation between Judaism and

Christianity. But still it was never cancelled from our sources, or rather not omitted when those were put into writing, which happened many years after the facts.

It cannot be said that Paul's text in *1 Thessalonians* 2:15, notwithstanding its harsh language, implies that all the Jews then and since are guilty of the death of Christ. However this text may be explained, it most certainly does not mean this. 'Deicide' has never been taught by the New Testament, nor the Christian Church as such, for that matter. Paul says very clearly in *1 Corinthians* 2:8: 'None of the rulers of this age knew the mystery: if they had known it, they would never have crucified the Lord of glory'. The same Paul is quite conscious that Jesus died 'because of our sins' (*Romans* 4:25), 'in accordance with the scriptures' (*1 Corinthians* 15:3). And at this theological level, it is us, the believers in Christ, who truly crucify him, then and again, when we are unfaithful to him. This was said, in scriptural terms, in the letter to the Hebrews (6:4–6) and taken up, to be learned by all concerned, in the *Catechism of the Council of Trent*. The passage in *Hebrews* to which the catechism text explicitly refers, may be quoted here: 'For when men have once been enlightened and have tasted the heavenly gift and become sharers in the Holy Spirit ... and then have fallen away, it is impossible to make them repent again, since they are crucifying the Son of God for themselves and holding him up to contempt'.

It is to be noted too that in the profession of faith, the *Credo*, which all Christians recite frequently – especially in the celebration of the central sacraments of the faith, baptism and the Eucharist – and which they hold as their distinctive mark, Jesus is said to have suffered 'under Pontius Pilate', with no mention being made of the Jews. This profession of faith, as is well known, comes from the very earliest times of the Christian Church.

This, of course, does not solve the historical question about who is responsible for what in the death of Jesus. Here, as you are well aware, there are different interpretations of the Gospel evidence, according to the different degrees of weight given by individual exegetes and Bible scholars. I shall not enter here into such a discussion. Suffice it to say that many interpreters, if not most, hold that some intervention of the Jewish leaders is required to adequately explain what is found in an admittedly difficult and much worked over account, which we know in three, if not four, different versions. It is also generally accepted that the final decision rested with the Roman procurator, the Jewish leaders being deprived at that time of the right of sentencing somebody to death. It must be added that it is not altogether clear (as sometimes said) that Pontius Pilate, as an irresolute weakling, was pushed or forced to the fateful decision of crucifying Jesus by an angry, excited Jewish mob. He was not that kind of man, according to what we know from other sources. He certainly knew what he was doing and did it with the conscious will of humiliating the Jews and their authorities: 'look at your king' (*John* 19:14) he says to them when he is about to condemn Jesus to death after having had him scourged. And exactly the same description he wanted written on the *titulus crucis* for all to see and ponder, refusing moreover to have it changed when the authorities ask him to do so: 'What I have written, I have written' (*John* 19:22).

It is this considered opinion which has been taken up by the Second Vatican Council in *Nostra Aetate* when it says: 'True, the Jewish authorities and those who followed their lead pressed for the death of Christ' (n. 4). But this is not to place any blame on the Jewish people as such, whether in that time or thereafter. Rather the contrary, because the Council goes on to say: 'still, what happened in his passion cannot be charged against all the Jews, without distinction, then alive, nor against the Jews of today'. Theologically this is a decisive statement, with magisterial, conciliar authority. It should lay to rest any controversy on this particular point still existing among Catholics.

This statement, which implies a certain reading of scripture and the scriptural data, gives us the key to interpret *Matthew* 27:25: 'let his blood be on us and our children'. Whatever the right meaning of this text (and the explanation for its presence only in *Matthew*), it is certainly not that all the Jews, till the end of time, if not converted, carry upon themselves the guilt for the death of Christ and are punished for it. For the same reason, it cannot be said, according to New Testament teaching, that all 'Jews' (that is, the Jewish people) stand under damnation and therefore are, again as such, rejected by God. The Council, also on this delicate point, has given us the clue for a correct reading of holy scripture, by saying: 'The Jews should not be presented as rejected or accused by God, as if this followed from the holy scriptures' (*Nostra Aetate*, n. 4). Negative and ambiguous texts, which seem to mean this, are to be read in the light of the general positive thrust of the New Testament regarding Judaism, to which I have referred above, but also in the light of more positive, unambiguous texts, which say the opposite, like *Romans* 9:1-5, already quoted, and *Romans* 11:1-2 ('I ask, then, has God rejected his people? Of course not ... no, God has not rejected his people whom he foreknew').

For the 'Jews' in the Gospel of *John*, some kind of anti-Judaism at some stage of the Gospel redaction would be admitted. That this is not at all the whole picture of Jews and Judaism in the Johannine Gospel is proved by the fact of the very positive references to be found in that Gospel. Some were quoted earlier, like *John* 4:22 - 'salvation comes from the Jews' - and others were alluded to. So, the picture is a mixed one, to say the least. On the other hand, it seems clear enough that, at the time of the final redaction of the Gospel, the community reflected and embodied in the last redaction considers itself a religious body different from Judaism and looks at it from outside. One should add here: and from a distance. A certain rift, and a painful one, for that matter, had certainly taken place some time before. It is quite possible, if not probable, that some sections of the Gospel reflect such hard feelings toward the 'mother' community from which nascent Christianity had dissociated itself, not without conflicts. This accounts for a certain measure of what I called 'anti-Judaism', in the Gospel of *John*. But I would insist that 'anti-Judaism', at least of this particular brand, is not exactly anti-Semitism in the senses spelled out at the beginning of this lecture.

However, such an 'anti-Judaism' could, and perhaps did, in the course of history, nurture the seeds of real anti-Semitic actions and prejudices. This is why we churchmen must be so careful to interpret rightly texts and terms and trends as those quoted, and keep a vigilant eye on what is done (or not done) around us in their presentation and explanation. I would submit that the same set of principles, *mutatis mutandis*, should be applied to a correct reading of the Gospel of *Matthew*.

Lastly, the Pharisees. Here I shall be very short. I am convinced, in fact, that from what can be known through sound scholarship, there is no question that the Pharisees, as such, were certainly not the hypocritical, repulsive bigots that a certain Christian (and also secular) tradition has made them to be. This is a caricature, and a very nasty one indeed. Again, one has only to look carefully at the text itself of the New Testament to find, alongside negative references, many positive ones. Gamaliel was a Pharisee (*Acts* 5:34) and so was Nicodemus (*John* 3:1; 19:39). The Pharisees warn Jesus that Herod is trying to kill him, and this in *Luke* (13:31), who is not kind to them. They are never mentioned in the actual account of the passion and crucifixion, while other groupings are frequently named. To convey of them a quite negative, almost diabolic picture, is unfair and unhistorical, whatever the failures of many or even most of them, which also the *Babylonian Talmud* recognises: of seven classes of Pharisees there described in a famous text, only one is approved of.

For this reason, the *Guidelines and Suggestions for the Implementation of 'Nostra Aetate'*, published by our Commission for Religious

Relations with the Jews in 1974, refers specifically either to the Pharisees and the 'Jews' in St John's Gospel and gives briefly some orientations on how to interpret these expressions rightly, so as to 'avoid appearing to arraign the Jewish people as such,' or the whole of the Pharisaic movement, whose rightful heir present Judaism considers itself to be.

Christ as Messiah

A third step could be made here, so as to give an answer to those who believe, for one reason or another, that the distinctive Christian profession of faith, namely the one in Jesus as Christ, or Messiah, is of itself anti-Semitic. They hold that such a profession would, in fact, imply almost automatically the depreciation of the Jewish religion: if it is said that the Messiah has already come, Judaism has no true right to exist. Therefore, all anti-Semitic prejudices are validated.

To this I would say the following. First, we must once again be careful not to jump from one set of assertions or convictions to another of an entirely different order. Professions of faith are one thing; social and even religious attitudes, especially if tinged with prejudices, are quite another. This is not to say that there might not be – and unfortunately there has been – a connection between one and the other. But the whole point is that this should not be so in the first place, and it raises a constant challenge to all our religions, as professed and lived out by their faithful, namely, to constantly keep a severe check on possible, but as such unwarranted, conclusions from what we believe or practice. This, I gather, is one of the major contributions of the Second Vatican Council, and not only in the field of Jewish/Christian relations.

Secondly, I would strongly argue that the affirmation just mentioned is simply not true. It does not follow from the Christian profession of faith that Judaism, let alone the Jewish people, is not worthy of any respect and that, in consequence, the door is wide open for anti-Semitism. The Christian profession of faith is a positive one: it looks to Jesus as the Christ. It does not refer to anything else. If it suggests a reference to Judaism, it is again a positive one, as said above, because it is from Judaism that we receive the notions of Messiah and messianism, and this establishes a link between both religions. It is a link which asks for reflection and deepening, pointing as it does to a kind of common hope, for Judaism is always hoping for the coming of the Messiah and/or the messianic age. For Christians, in fact, if the Messiah has already come, it is also an article of our profession of faith that he is nonetheless expected in a second coming. Thus the Christ-Messiah links us to Judaism, because he was and remains a Jew, and with him Judaism enters into Christianity through the main door.

Yes, we Christians are utterly convinced that this Christ, whose human identity we receive from Judaism, is since his resurrection the Lord and centre of world and history. We believe him to be the Son of God. This, of course, divides us from Judaism. We must say then that the same Jesus who brings us together divides us. This is true, and there is no point in blurring the distinction. Nevertheless, the fact of our link remains for ever, and this means that even in our separation, we are mysteriously 'linked' together, as *Nostra Aetate* says in the first sentence of the section on Judaism (n. 4). This means that, far from being intrinsically anti-Semitic, the Christ is, so to speak, intrinsically pro-Semitic, and properly understood leads not to depreciation of the Jewish people or the Jewish religion, but, on the contrary, to a deep appreciation of both. Very deep, in fact, because it is grounded not in any external conjunctural circumstance of some kind, but in the very distinctive identity of Christianity. It cannot be said, therefore, that Christianity, as a normative body of belief and practice embodied in the New Testament, is anti-Semitic. The question of our title, thus far, must therefore be answered in the negative.

Anti-Semitic interpretations of Christianity

I would not like, however, to seem to dodge a further question. If Christianity as such is not anti-Semitic (in the first of the three senses listed above) could it perhaps be said that Christianity is or has been proved to be anti-Semitic in any of the two other meanings? Here one has to be very honest, and acknowledge quite openly:

- that some and perhaps many interpretations of Christianity along the ages have been unjust and prejudiced against Judaism;
- that sometimes such misguided interpretations have been translated into practice, legal or otherwise, seriously discriminating, attacking, oppressing, and even violently mishandling Jews, to the point of physical suppression;
- that this has obviously nourished, in the Graeco-Roman world, a form of anti-Semitism, coming from pre-Christian sources, to which, for instance Josephus Flavius (*Contra Appionem*) and Philo (*Legatio ad Caium*) refer to. But it has also quickly developed into a form of anti-Semitism of its own.

Now, having acknowledged all this and even more that could and should be acknowledged, I would like to state very clearly that a careful distinction must be drawn between this kind of 'Christianity' – or perhaps 'Christendom' – and the more fundamental, basic meaning of the same word, to which I have been referring up till now. The Christian body of belief and practice is one thing; historical and cultural realisations of that body of belief and practice are quite another. It must be admitted, therefore, that most if not all historical embodiments of Christianity – this side of history – do not easily live up, socially and culturally, to the requirements of our own religious profession. In this, I fear, we are not alone. I wonder if any other religion, in the course of history, has been able to create in its own geographical context a world entirely faithful to its ideals.

Christianity, however, is a very special case in this connection, because I do not think it has been given to any other religion (not even Islam) as it has been given to us, to rule and mould and give a shape for such a protracted period in history to such an important section of humanity. A mixed blessing, indeed. One can point to many achievements, no doubt; but deficiencies and limitations only appear thus in a more painful light. Our only excuse, if any, is that men and women are very seldom up to the task assigned them by the very faith they profess and profess sincerely. This is why we Catholics value so much our saints. In a way they atone for the weakness of the rest. Some very nasty forms of anti-Semitism are part of such deficiencies. It is a grace of God that we are now much more aware of them. But it is a greater grace still that we are convinced, or perhaps beginning to be convinced, that our own identity (Christianity in the first meaning listed above) not only does not approve of such deviations, but positively condemns them and requires of us to go the opposite way, namely, to love, respect and, if need be, help and protect our Jewish brother.

When all this is said and done, I think there is still room to show that, notwithstanding our negative record, some trends at least of what Christianity really means for Judaism have persisted along the ages, even in the darkest moments. I shall only mention here a few points, without entering into any deep analysis. But I am convinced that careful historico-theological analysis could bear them up and perhaps even add some other.

Firstly, the notion, however dim, of a certain debt to Judaism has never been lost in the Christian tradition. This indebtedness has perhaps been interpreted in the wrong way, but the trend was there and it is partly on this basis that the present change has been built. I add that the consciousness of this debt has been particularly alive in liturgy and in biblical scholarship. Examples would be easy to find for both.

There has always been a clear conviction, at least at the theological and juridical levels of the Church, and therefore in the places where decisions are made, that, for instance, Jews should not be baptised against their will, and this goes as far back as St Gregory the Great (end of the sixth century). Additionally, there was no excuse for wantonly killing Jews, or otherwise oppressing them physically, much less exterminating them. Popes and prelates and saints, like St Bernard, vigorously opposed the massacre of Jews by crusaders on their way to the east. Popes have also strongly condemned the so-called 'blood libel', namely the perverse idea that Jews needed the blood of a Christian infant or boy for the Easter rites and murdered them in consequence. The cult of such imaginary 'martyrs' was never approved of and at times severely disapproved, like, in the case of Simon of Trent, by Sixtus IV, or, for a similar case in Poland, by Benedict XIV.

Further, I would add to this that condemnations of anti-Semitism, in the more modern 'racist' variety, had been expressed in the Catholic Church before the Second Vatican Council. I shall only mention in this connection the decree of the Congregation of the Holy Office on 28 March 1928, under Pius XI, explicitly condemning anti-Semitism under that name in a context which seemingly refers more to France than to Weimar Germany. The same Pius XI dedicated a whole encyclical to the evil of racism, and to bring the point home did not hesitate to have it published in German, contrary to the time honoured Roman preference for Latin. The 1937 encyclical, *Mit brennender Sorge*, was preceded by a whole series of instructions and orientations by Holy See offices about how to counter in Catholic education the dangers of racist theories, which then meant in the first place anti-Semitism. It was the same Pius XI who said in September 1938 to a group of Belgian journalists: 'we refer, in the eucharistic prayer of the Mass, to Abraham our father in faith; thus we are all, spiritually, Semites'. The opposition to anti-Semitism, then rampant, is obvious. If anything, such reactions prove the truth of the central assertion of this lecture: Christianity is not anti-Semitic.

But, as an appropriate conclusion to this lecture, I feel I should go a step further. It is not enough just to say that Christianity is not anti-Semitic. Whatever our historical record, and I am well aware of the deficiencies of men and women of the Catholic faith, in this point (as in others) I must say here that Christianity and anti-Semitism as this word is understood today are intrinsically incompatible. Anti-Semitism, therefore, is simply anti-Christian. This, I believe, is the real decisive thrust of all I have had to say.

Cardinal Joseph Ratzinger (1988)
CONSUMER MATERIALISM AND CHRISTIAN HOPE

In modern literature, the graphic arts, cinema and theatre, a predominantly gloomy picture of man is the fashion. What is sublime and noble is suspect from the start; it has to be yanked off its pedestal and seen for what it is. Morality is only hypocrisy, happiness no more than self-deception. Suspicion is the authentically moral stance; unmasking deception is its greatest achievement. Criticising society is a duty; indeed the dangers which threaten us cannot be shown with sufficient cruelty and violence. It is true that this disposition towards the negative is not without limits. There is also a duty at the same time to optimism which cannot be offended without paying the price. Should anyone, for example, venture the opinion that not everything in the spiritual development of modernity may be correct, that in some essential areas it may be necessary to return and reflect upon the common wisdom of the great cultures, obviously he has chosen the wrong kind of criticism. For he finds himself confronted all at once by a determined defence of the fundamental judgements of modernity, namely that the basic line of historical development is progress and thus the good lies in the future, nowhere else; and not all the delight in negativity may seriously call this into question.

The particular discord within modern social criticism clearly becomes manifest in the radically contradictory responses with which prevailing opinion reacted to the two events which were perceived last year as being the starkest moral challenges to our society. The first was the misfortune of Chernobyl. Those who would be considered enlightened could not describe the danger of these events in terms drastic enough. They had to see a colossal menace looming over all living things and only the complete abandonment of atomic energy could be the right answer to it. The other event was the rapid advance of the new viral disease, AIDS. There is no doubt that many more people will become sick and die from AIDS than have already died in the wake of Chernobyl, and that the danger posed by this new scourge of mankind stands nearer the door of each individual than does the peril presented by nuclear power plants. Nonetheless, whoever dares to say that mankind ought to refrain from that inordinate sexual licence which gives AIDS its effective power is put on the sidelines as a hopeless obscurantist because of his public attitude. Such an idea can only be deplored and passed over in silence by the enlightened of today. From all of this, it is apparent that there are today permissible and forbidden types of social criticism. The permissible kind, however, goes no further than to the threshold of society's fundamental judgements which may not be put into question.

The moral problems of our time – an attempt at diagnosis
The topic which I have chosen certainly requires the kind of reflection which will not be intimidated by such a taboo. To be sure, it would be an incorrect turn-around to view our society, and its moral situation all told, in shades of darkest grey alone. We should not allow ourselves to be influenced by the superficial duty to optimism imposed by certain trends. But even less should we succumb to the temptation to ignore the positive elements in the make-up of our time. Naturally, it cannot be our purpose here to give an exhaustive account of the moral figure cast by our age. Our reflection intends to locate that which is supportive and healing, that basic guideline by which one can live through the present and thus unlock the door to the future. We are inquiring about the characteristic elements of our time so we can learn what hinders access to the right way and what helps it. And so, I am not speaking in this first part of my analysis about defects or virtues, which there have always been and probably

always will be. We are dealing rather with the characteristic signs of our time. On the negative side, two elements catch our eye, elements which do not belong to other epochs in the same way: terrorism and drugs. In a positive vein, there is a strong moral consciousness exerting its influence, a consciousness which focuses essentially upon values in the social sphere: freedom for the downtrodden, solidarity with the poor and the disadvantaged, peace and reconciliation.

The problem of drugs

Let us try to consider these phenomena with a closer look. I remember an argument which I had with several friends in Ernst Bloch's home. The discussion had come by chance to the problem of drugs which then – the late 1960s – was first beginning to make its appearance. Someone asked how it could be that this temptation should suddenly crop up and why, for example, it apparently did not arise in the Middle Ages. Everybody was agreed that it would not be sufficient to answer that the areas of cultivation then were just too far removed. Phenomena like the appearance of drug abuse are not to be explained by such superficial circumstances. They originate from deeper needs or wants upon which depends the further problem of providing for them too. And so I ventured the thesis that there was obviously not that spiritual emptiness then which one seeks to fill with drugs; or, in other words, the thirst of the heart, of the inner man, found an answer then which made drugs unnecessary. I still remember the shocked indignation with which Mrs Bloch reacted to this suggested solution. From the vision of history which dialectical materialism had given, it was next to sacrilege for her to think that bygone ages might have been superior to our own in matters of more than little consequence. In the Middle Ages, which were a time of oppression and religious prejudices, it was impossible that the deprived masses lived happier lives of interior harmony than in our time which has already advanced some distance along the road of liberation. The whole logic of 'liberation' would thus collapse. How then is the process to be explained? The question remained without an answer that evening.

Considering that I do not subscribe to the worldview of materialism, I maintain that my thesis from that time on has been ever more vindicated. But it does have to be concretised. In this regard, the thought of Ernst Bloch could ever offer a helpful start. For Bloch, the world of fact is evil. The hope principle means that man energetically opposes facts. He recognises himself as obliged to overcome the evil world of facts in order to create a better world. I would say that drug abuse is a form of protest against facts. The one who resorts to drugs refuses to come to terms with the world of facts. He looks for a better world. Drugs are the result of despairing of a world which is experienced as a prison built of facts in which man cannot long endure. Naturally many other things enter here as well: the search for adventure, going along with the crowd, what others do, the enterprise of pushers and so on. But the heart of it still is the revolt against a reality perceived as a prison. The grand 'trip' which people look for in drugs is a perversion of mysticism, the warping of the human desire for immortality, the 'no' to the impossibility of overcoming the immanent, and the attempt to enfold the limits of one's own being in the eternal. The patient and humble adventure of asceticism, which, step by step, climbs nearer to the God who is coming down to meet man, finds itself replaced by the power of magic – that is, the magic key of drugs – the moral and religious path is set aside for that of technology. Drugs are the pseudo-mysticism of a world which no longer believes but which cannot for all that shake off the yearning of the soul for paradise. Drugs are therefore a warning signal with deep reverberations: they not only reveal the vacuum in our society which its instruments cannot remedy; they point to an interior longing in man which breaks out in perverted form if it does not find its true satisfaction.

Terrorism as a moral problem

The point of departure for terrorism is closely related to that of drugs. Here too we find initially a protest against the world as it is and the demand for a better one. Terrorism is in its roots a kind of 'moralism', to be sure a misdirected moralism which turns into a cruel parody of the true aims and methods of the moral person. It is no accident that terrorism has had its beginnings in the universities and among young people drawing fresh, heightened inspiration from religious thought, here again, in the context of modern theology. Terrorism was, in the first instance, a religious enthusiasm diverted to earthly concerns, a messianic expectation translated into political fanaticism. Belief in the hereafter had been shattered or in any case had become irrelevant. The yardstick of other-worldly hope, however, was not given up. It was applied instead to the present world. God was no longer looked upon as one really acting in history; but, as in the past and indeed from the beginning, the fulfilment of his promises was still sought after. 'God has no other arms than our own' – that meant that now the redemption of these promises can and must be taken care of by ourselves. Loathing for the spiritual and emotional emptiness in our society, longing for the wholly-other, the claim to an unconditional salvation without limits or restrictions – this is the religious component, in a manner of speaking, within the phenomenon of terrorism. It is this religious component which gave terrorism the momentum of a passion which goes to any length, which gave it its uncompromising stance and its pretence to the idealistic. All this becomes quite dangerous based as it is upon the decisive worldliness of its messianic hope: the unconditional is required from what is contingent, the eternal from what is finite. This internal contradiction points out the real tragedy of the phenomenon in which the sublime vocation of human beings is transformed into an instrument of the great deception, the 'big lie'.

The lie within the promise of terrorism, however, was hidden from its average participant because of the alliance between religious expectation and the spirit of the modern intellectual. This consists first of all in the halting of all traditional norms of morality before the tribunal of positivist reason, getting to the bottom of them and proving them to be unfounded. Morality does not lie in present existence but in the future. Man has to fashion himself. The only moral value there is lies in the future of society when we will get everything we do not have now. Morality in the present consists in working for the sake of this future society. The new standard of morality says, then: whatever serves the bringing about of this new society is moral. And what serves it can be determined by the scientific methods of political strategy, psychology, and sociology. The 'moral' becomes the 'scientific': morality no longer has a 'phantom' goal - heaven - but a realisable phenomenon, the new age. In this way the moral and the religious have become realistic and 'scientific'. What more does one want? Is it any wonder that sincerely idealistic young people have felt themselves challenged by such promises?

Only from this closer perspective can one see the devil's foot upon the whole business and hear the sneer of Mephistopheles: 'The future creates what is moral'. By this standard even murder can be 'moral'; on the way to humanity even the inhuman has to serve. This is basically the same logic which states that for 'really top-notch scientific results' even embryos may sometimes be sacrificed. And it is the same concept of freedom which lectures us that it ought to lie within the realm of woman's personal choice to destroy a child who stands in the way of her self-fulfilment. Thus, terrorism proceeds undiminished upon somewhat more sublime battlefields today with the full blessing of science and the enlightened spirit. True, the brutal terrorism of those who would change society has been condemned in western countries: it has too greatly threatened the habits of life in these societies and the immorality of its morality has become all too conspicuous. But a real prevention of its root causes has not yet taken place. One can even look at it in such a way as to remain untroubled by its outbreak in the faraway lands of the third world which lie at a safe remove from us. And still, as before, it is practically immoral not to recommend the typical slogans for the third world, even if one might not gladly see them applied in one's own circumstances. Partisanship for militant liberationist ideologies appears as a kind of moral compromise in the sense that one allows things to go well for oneself and would like to see nothing essential changed. The practice of terrorism, thank goodness, has been extensively reduced in Europe once more. Its spiritual foundations, however, have not been overturned, and, as long as this is so, it can erupt anew at any time.

The new turning towards morality and religion

And so the question comes to be framed in a positive way: what is the true converse to those spiritual foundations which we have outlined so briefly? Where exactly does the defect lie? Before we get to the bottom of this question, however, we have to complete our stock-taking of present day society. We said that there were two outstanding negative phenomena, the advancement of drug abuse and the threat of terrorism, and that there was, on the other hand, a positive phenomenon as well, an intense, new desire for moral values like freedom, justice, and peace. Can an answer to the menace of our age possibly come forth from this? First of all, we have to determine whether these values, out of all those on the horizon, are largely identical with the values which the champions of the movements of violence have proclaimed and hail as their goals. Abuse, of course, does not discredit the value as such. What is new among numbers of young people today is that these goals are now projected upon the plane of concrete political and social action, and thus they are stripped of their irrational and violent character. Ideologies have been cast aside and so one can directly recognise what is good once more. In point of fact, this may be welcomed as an element of hope: God's profound message can be smothered and distorted in man. Nonetheless, it is constantly bursting forth anew, working a way out for itself. Also pertinent in this context is the fact that a new yearning for recollection, for contemplation, for the truly sacred, indeed for contact with God, is becoming evident.

To this extent energies have been coming forth which permit us to have hope. But just as the source has to be tapped so that its waters do not simply ooze away, so the impulses of purification and order are required so that these energies come to have their true effect. The new religious aspiration can easily be deflected into the esoteric. It can evaporate in sheer romanticism. There are two ever-present hurdles difficult for it to get over: it seems hard to take on the continuity of a permanent discipline, a straight way, which does not allow itself a detour from the primary road of the will and intellect for a quick gratification of one's feelings. Even harder than this appears the channelling of such desire into the communion of life of an 'institution' of faith, in which religion as faith has become the way and the form of a community. Where this double hurdle is not overcome, though, religion degenerates into a pleasurable escape and exhibits no community and no moral power which obliges the individual. Reason and will quit its service; all that is left, then, is feeling, and that is too little.

These new moral impulses are likewise threatened in the same way. Their exposed flank is the widespread defect in the values of individualistic ethics. The vision is directed towards the large scale and the totality. Certainly it should be recognised that the turning to fringe groups is often an expression of a personal willingness to help which discharges the desire to serve and be of assistance in wondrously worthy ways. On the whole, however, this is to be viewed rather as a weakness in one's personal and motivational make-up. It is easier to demonstrate for the rights and freedom of one's own group than to practise in everyday life the discipline of freedom and the patience of love for those who suffer, or to bind oneself for all of life to such service with the sacrifice of the greater part of one's individual freedoms. It is astonishing that the desire to serve has been visibly and decisively weakened in the Church too: religious communities, dedicated to the care of the sick and elderly, attract hardly any new vocations. The preference is to engage in more ambitious 'pastoral' ministries. But what is really more 'pastoral' than an unpretentious life lived in service to those who are suffering? For these kinds of service, though, there is an important professional credential required - without a deep moral and religious foundation, they get frozen into mere technical procedures and no longer perform what is crucial for the human being.

The weak side of the present moral starting point lies first of all in the feebleness of individual ethics' ability to motivate. Something deeper lies behind this: moral values have lost their evidence in a technological society and, as a result, any compelling claim they may have had as well. They are everyone's objectives for which one may be enthusiastic, even passionate. But it is not reasonable that they place an obligation on me, if the effect on me would be negative, if my own freedom and personal happiness are thereby threatened. These objectives therefore are generally ineffective and the public *élan* with which they are given prominence and steadfastly defended in various speeches is probably compensation for the failure to realise them in the concrete. And so we have come back once more to the question we posed as to where exactly the defect begins in that type of moralism which ends up in terrorism. Because this defect is also the real root to almost all the other problems of our time, its implications reach far beyond the areas haunted by terrorists.

Elements of a response

The essence of morality

Let us try to make our way gradually towards the facts of the case. I said that what is moral has lost its evidence. Only a small number of people in modern society will believe in the existence of commandments come from God; and still fewer are convinced that these commandments – if there are such – are handed down without error through the Church, through the religious community. The idea that another's will, the Creator's will, has a call upon us and that our being becomes as it should be through the harmony of our will with his will is a concept foreign to a great part of mankind. In any case, the function of having put the 'big bang' into operation remains odd for God. The idea of his being active in our midst or of man being under his will seems to most to be a naïvely anthropomorphic image of the divine by which man himself is over-rated. Now the concept of a personal relationship between God and Creator and each individual person is certainly not missing from the religious and moral history of humanity; but it is limited in its pure form to the realm of biblical religion. What was first of all common to all of pre-modern mankind, however, lies really along the self-same line: the conviction that in man's being there lies an imperative, the conviction that man does not devise morality itself by calculating expediencies; rather he comes upon it in the being of things.

Long before the outbreak of terrorism and the invasion of drugs, the English author and philosopher, C S Lewis, called attention to the grievous danger of the abolition of man which lies in the collapse of the foundations of morality. He thus gave stress to humankind's justification upon which the continuance of man as man depends. Lewis shows the continuance of this justification with a glance at all the great civilisations. He refers not only to the moral heritage of the Greeks and its particular articulation by Plato,

Aristotle and the Stoa. These intended to lead man to an awareness of reason in his being and from that to insist upon the cultivation of 'his kinship of being with reason'. Lewis also recalls the idea of the Rta in early Hinduism, which asserts the harmony of the cosmic order, the moral virtues and the temple rituals. He underscores in a special way the Chinese doctrine of the Tao: 'It is nature, it is the way, the road. It is the way in which the universe goes on. ... It is also the way in which every man should tread in imitation of that cosmic and supercosmic progression, conforming all activities to that great exemplar' (*The Abolition of Man*). Lewis refers as well to the law of Israel, which unites cosmos and history and intends above all to be the expression of the truth about man as much as the truth about the world.

An appreciation of the great civilisations discloses differences in detail, but starker by far than these differences is the great common strain which reveals itself as early evidence of the human business of living: the teaching of objective values which are manifest in the being of the world; the belief that there are attitudes which are true in accord with the message of the 'All', and therefore good, and that there are other attitudes as well which are contrary to being and thus are wrong for good and for all.

Modern mankind has been persuaded that human moral values are radically opposed one to another in the same way that religious are. In both cases the simple conclusion is drawn that all of these are human inventions whose absurdity we can finally detect and replace with reasonable knowledge. This diagnosis, though, is extremely superficial. It hooks on to a series of details which are set up in random fashion, one next to the other, and so it arrives at the banality of its superior insight. The reality is that the fundamental intuition concerning the moral character of being itself and the necessity for harmony between human existence and the message of nature is common to all the great civilisations; and thus the great moral imperatives are also a possession held in common. C S Lewis expressed this emphatically when he said:

> *This thing, which I have called for convenience the Tao, and which others may call natural law, or traditional morality, or the first principle of practical reason, or the first platitudes, is not one among a series of possible systems of value. It is the sole source of all value judgements. If it is rejected, all value is rejected. If any value is retained, it is retained. The effort to refute it and to raise a new system of value in its place is self-contradictory.*

The creation of pseudo-science: the abolition of man

The problem of modernity, the moral problem of our time, consists in the fact that it has separated itself from this primeval testimony. In order truly to understand the process, we have to describe it in yet greater detail. It is characteristic of the scientific mind to create an abyss between the world of feelings and the world of facts. Feelings are subjective, facts are objective. 'Facts', i.e. those things which can be determined outside of ourselves, are still and all just 'facts', bare-boned details. To add to the atom over and above its mathematical determinations some further properties of, let us say, a moral or aesthetic nature is looked upon as imagination simply gone wild. This reduction of nature to demonstrable and thus pliable facts has consequences: no moral message outside of ourselves can reach us any more. The moral, just as much as the religious, belongs to the realm of the subjective; it has no place in the objective. If it is subjective, it is the composition of man. It does not precede us; we precede it and create it.

This movement of 'objectification', which 'gets to the bottom' of things and renders them manageable, recognises no limit to its being. A Comte had already put forth a principle for a kind of physics of human beings. Little by little the most difficult object of nature should become understandable to science, that is, be subjected to scientific knowledge - this most difficult object being man. Man will then be as well understood as matter already is.

Psychoanalysis and sociology are the fundamental tools for making good this postulate. One can now (so it appears) explain the mechanisms by which man came to the belief that nature might express a moral law. It is true: the completely transparent man is no longer a man at all. By the nature of such perception he can only be a mere detail; 'To "see through" all things is the same as not to see', Lewis noted. The theories of evolution crafted upon an all-embracing worldview seal the fate of this kind of vision and also try to compensate for it. Of course, as they say, there is no logic to anything or, more correctly, everything is the way it is because of the simple logic of facts.

One can even reconstruct now the purely mechanical course of the world's development in the perfect doctrine of evolution with its theories of chance and necessity. 'Evolution' makes the inference that imitation of its successes should be the new morality: the goal of evolution is survival and the perfection of the species. The optimal survival for the species 'man', then, would be the basic moral value; and the rules one makes accordingly to achieve this would be the only moral system. It is only apparent that this represents a return to eavesdropping upon the moral wisdom of nature. In reality, God's dominion is now meaningless, for evolution coming forth from itself is meaningless. It is the calculus of probabilities and power which are now in control. Morality has been eroded and man as human being has worn away with it. It is no longer prudent to ask why one should hold fast to this kind of survival.

Once more I would like to have C S Lewis put in a word. He saw this process already in 1943 and described it with keen accuracy. He discerns in it the old compact with the magician:

Give up our soul, get power in return. But once our souls, that is, our selves, have been given up the power thus conferred will not belong to us. ... It is in man's power to treat himself as a mere 'natural object'. ... The real objection is that if man chooses to treat himself as raw material, raw material he will be: not raw material to be manipulated, as he fondly imagined, by himself, but by mere appetite, that is, mere nature, in the person of his dehumanised conditioners.

Lewis raised this warning during the Second World War because he saw how, with the destruction of morality, the very capacity to defend his nation against the onslaught of barbarism was imperilled. He was objective enough, though, to add the following: 'I am not here thinking solely, perhaps not even chiefly, of those who are our public enemies at the moment. The process which, if not checked, will abolish man, goes on apace among communists and democrats, no less than among fascists.' This seems to me to be a comment of great import: the opposing worldviews of today, have a common starting point in the rejection of the natural moral law and the reduction of the world to 'mere' acts. The measure with which they illogically hold on to the old values differs, but, at their core, they are threatened with the same peril.

The real falsehood in that worldview, for which drugs and terrorism are but the symptoms, consists in its reduction of the world to facts and in the narrowing of reason to quantitative perception. The essential in man is shoved off into the subjective and so into the unreal. The 'abolition of man' which follows from making absolute one method of coming to knowledge is the clear distortion of this worldview as well. We have man; and whoever feels compelled, on the basis of some theory he has, to pull him off into the realm of transparent, prefabricated devices, lives with a narrowed perception which what is essential hastens to oppose. If science aims for the most comprehensive knowledge in accord with reality possible, then to make absolute one method is the opposite of science. This means, in other words, that practical reason too, upon which true moral knowledge depends, is a real form of reason and not merely the expression of subjective feelings not worth knowing. We have to learn how to appreciate once again that the great moral insights of mankind are just as reasonable and true, indeed truer, than experimental findings in the realm of science and technology. They are truer because they touch more deeply upon the reality of being and they are more crucial for the existence of humanity.

The reason of morality and the reason of faith
Two conclusions emerge from this. The first is that the moral imperative is not man's imprisonment from which he must make his escape in order finally to be able to do as he wants. The moral imperative constitutes man's dignity and if he gets rid of it he does not become freer. Rather, he has stepped back into the world of mere devices, of things. If there is no longer an imperative to which he can and should respond in freedom, then actually there is no range for freedom any more. Moral knowledge is the true content of human dignity; but one does not come to this knowledge without at the same time experiencing it as an obligation upon one's freedom. Morality is not man's prison; it is rather the divine in him.

To illustrate the second conclusion, we have to recall once more the fundamental insight we came to previously: practical (or moral) reason is reason in its highest sense, for it delves deeper into the true mystery or reality than does experimental reason. This means, however, that Christian faith is not a limitation or a handicap for reason. Instead it liberates it at the very start for its own work. Practical reason also needs the guarantee of an experiment, but a greater kind of experiment than can be conducted in the laboratory. It requires the experiment of successful human existence which can come only with subsequent history itself. For this reason, practical reason was always ordered towards the grand enterprise of experiencing and testing the collective visions of ethics and religion. Just as science, on one hand, depends upon the brilliant breakthroughs of great individuals, so, on the other hand, the construction of a systematic ethic depends upon the particular vision of individuals who were given a glimpse of the whole. The grand ethical developments of Greece and of the Near and Far East, about which we spoke a moment ago, have forfeited nothing in terms of the validity which lies at the heart of their assertions. We may look upon them now, however, as tributaries, which flow towards the grand river of Christianity and its explanation of reality.

Actually, the moral vision of Christian faith is not something particularly Christian; it is rather the synthesis of the great moral intuitions of humanity from a new centre which holds them all together. This concurrence of ethical wisdom is raised many times today as an argument against the binding force of the commandments delivered by God in the scriptures. One can see, so the argument goes, that the Bible does not really possess a moral wisdom, but that from time to time it adopted as its own the moral insights of the world around it. Therefore, the authority in morality would be just that which at some time in a particular age was recognised as reasonable. One has come already, then, to the cramming of morality into a simple calculus, that is, to the abolition of the moral in the real sense of the term.

It is just the opposite which is correct: the inner coherence of morality's fundamental direction, which has gradually been purified as it develops, is the best proof of its validity – the best proof, that it is discovered, not devised. Discovered – how? Here the realms of revelation and reason mesh closely with one another. These insights are discovered by some, as we said, through particular figures who made it possible to see more deeply. We call such seeing, which goes above and beyond one's own acquisition of knowledge, revelation.

What is seen in the ethical realm, however, is essentially that same moral message which lies in creation itself. For nature is not, as science in an ivory tower would have it, a kind of montage put together by chance and the laws of probability; rather, it is creation. In nature the creator Spirit expresses himself. For this reason, there are not only natural laws in the sense of physical functions; there is the actual law of nature which is a moral law. Creation itself teaches us how we can be human beings in the proper way. The Christian faith, which helps us to recognise creation as creation, is not a handicap for reason. It gives practical reason room for growth and development. The moral law which the Church teaches is not a special burden for Christians but man's defence against the attempt to reduce him to nothing. If morality – as we say – is not the enslavement but the liberation of man, then the Christian faith is the outpost of human freedom.

Man needs ethos in order to be himself. Ethos, however, requires belief in creation and immortality: that is, it requires the objectivity of the imperative and its ultimate redemption by responsibility and fulfilment. The impossibility of a human existence cut off from this is indirect proof for the truth of the Christian faith and its hope. This hope is a saving hope for human beings, even still today. The Christian may be happy in his faith; without the glad tidings of faith, mankind cannot endure in the long run. The joy of faith is its responsibility: we should lay hold of it with fresh courage in this moment of our history.

Archbishop Derek Worlock (1995)
WHAT THE BUTLER DID NOT SEE:
THE CHANGING FACE OF EDUCATION

When, some weeks ago, I saw that I had been invited to deliver the final address at this important national conference on Catholic education, I asked myself what on earth the organisers might be expecting of me, once all your ecclesiastical, educational and catechetical experts had had their 'go'. Was it just to fill a gap before the final Mass? Was the invitation based on my entertainment value, after the delegates had packed everything of consequence, including their notebooks, and been told to vacate their bedrooms? Or was it another round of the episcopal 'antiques roadshow', to which for some time now I have been asked to contribute from my store of anecdote and reminiscence?

At least, at this stage in your conference, no-one has asked me to give the now increasingly popular 'keynote address'. At a recent conference I was asked to deliver such on the opening evening, only to discover that there were four more 'keynotes' the following day. I have not been here long enough to synthesise the earlier wisdom and to sum it all up for you this morning; and my apprehension increased when I read in the original draft programme that I was to speak of the development of Catholic education since the 1944 Act. How many hours had been allocated to me? So I decided to settle for reminiscence, with some relevant features and some contrasts and I pleaded for a change of title accordingly. So here goes.

In a few weeks time it will be fifty years ago since I first occupied the Private Secretary's desk at Archbishop's House, Westminster. VE had just passed; the atom bomb and VJ were still ahead. A caretaker government had taken over from the all-party National Government, led by Churchill since the 'amazing summer' of 1940;

and a General Election, which would sweep the Tories from power, was proximate. Mr R A Butler had moved from the Board of Education to the Ministry of Labour; but the talk was all of post-war reconstruction. If the main concern of the nation was with the social implications of the Beveridge report, for the Catholic Church the question of parents' rights and Catholic schools was near the top of the agenda.

A new Archbishop, Bernard Griffin, fresh from child welfare concerns in Birmingham, and from the role of Air Raid Warden and Auxiliary Bishop, had been named *Praeses Perpetuus Angliae et Cambriae.* He had succeeded the great old Yorkshireman, Arthur Hinsley, whose thundering war-time broadcasts had made him a national hero. The new Archbishop of Westminster had been entrusted with the difficult task of trying to unite a hierarchy, doubly split - north and south, Irish and English - and also of trying to regain the confidence and leadership of the Catholic body, clerical and lay, in order to represent its interests to the public authorities. It was clear that the government had preferred to deal with certain of the Roman Catholic members of the hereditary peerage. The situation had not been helped when the aged Viscount Fitzalan had confided to Mr Butler that he did not trust Archbishop Downey, the soporous but reluctant interim leader of the hierarchy after Cardinal Hinsley's death. The somewhat critical London laity, who had favoured a more local candidate for Westminster, were further affronted when, soon after arriving in the metropolis and smarting beneath the suggestion that he was merely 'from the provinces', the unfortunate Griffin blotted his copybook with the pundits by referring to the City of Westminster as one of the 'suburbs' of London. Uneasy times at which to be negotiating the future of Catholic schools.

I must confess that at that time, in my seminary preparing for priestly ordination, much of this passed me by. But not for long.

Within a year, the authorities mislaid the health warning which should have been attached to my ordination certificate and, armed with a *London A-Z*, I was installed as part of the new regime at Westminster. I recall very well my first morning at the Private Secretary's desk at Archbishop's House. My predecessor had offered me only one bit of advice:'If the Pope arrives, put him in the waiting room'. But it was the phone which rang first. I raised the receiver carefully in time to hear a foreign accent saying, 'Chinese Embassy here'. I nearly made a dreadful mistake, for I was convinced that it must be a school-friend of mine who frequently delighted in picking up the phone when it rang and announcing himself as 'Chinese laundry'. But before I could reply in kind, the voice asked,'Could the Ambassador, Dr Wellington Koo, call to see the Archbishop?' I promised to ring back and started a list of names which I must mention to the Archbishop. This I would do when he was free from entertaining a bishop who had arrived to give evidence to a tribunal preparing for the beatification of a Mother Foundress, and who had already asked me if that afternoon I would show him the blue-behinded baboons in the London Zoo in Regent's Park. (Marvel, if you will, at my recollection of detail. Not for nothing have I been called the memory-bank of the Bishops' Conference!)

It was the second phone-call that morning which was the more relevant to this conference. I reached for my notepad, picked up the receiver, and recited, 'Victoria 4717: this is the Archbishop's Private Secretary'. To this I received the cheerful rejoinder, 'And this is 10 Downing Street, the Prime Minister's Secretary'. I hesitated - well, wouldn't you? Then the voice went on, 'This is Major Desmond Morton, Father. I gather that your boss wants to speak to my boss. Do you know what about?' I admitted that I did not but I would try to find out. I decided that, visiting bishop and Monkey Hill or not, I had better deliver that message at once, and an equally cheerful Archbishop told me to tell Desmond Morton, 'Education'. This was duly conveyed to Downing Street and it was not long before Morton was back on the phone. 'Look here,' he said, 'I told the PM that the Archbishop wanted to see him, and, as I expected, he asked "what about?" But when I told him, "Education", he replied, "That's the one thing I don't want to talk to him about. That's Rab's thing."'

You should note that by then the caretaker government had taken over, Butler had already moved to the Ministry of Labour, and only a few weeks later when the general election count took place during the Potsdam Conference, both men and the government were out of office. (It was an astonishing reversal of fortune, marked in my memory by the fact that I had to accompany my Archbishop that evening to a dinner at the Dorchester Hotel. In the reception area was a blackboard, like a cricket scoreboard showing that the National Government's lead of about 200 in the previous innings had melted away and that now the Labour Party was 146 ahead. Seated in that foyer amidst an air of gloom sat the bewildered batsmen and their wives who had been skittled out. The final sign of change came during the soup course. I was sitting opposite the afore-mentioned Viscount Fitzalan - in his more cheerful moments a picture of gloom - for whom Stoker Wally Edwards, MP of Stepney, about to become Civil Lord of Admiralty, pulled out of his pocket a packet of ten Players cigarettes and said, ''ere, 'ave a fag'.) The age of the Butler Education Act had arrived.

Those of you who have had the privilege of occupying the waiting room outside the office of the Minister or Secretary of State for Education, will doubtless recall that one of the walls is now almost covered with photographs of successive but previous holders of that office, post-Butler, from Ellen Wilkinson to John Patten. It is an impressive collection of Parliamentarians, many of whom are memorable, though with the possible exception of Kenneth Baker and his 'days' none other than Butler has bequeathed his or her name to educational legislation.

We should be deeply grateful to the Catholic Record Society for its inclusion in its issue of *Recusant History* for October 1994 of an article by John Davies entitled '*L'Art du Possible*', comprising for the most part correspondence and records of negotiations involving the Board of Education and the Catholic Church over the White Paper and the Education Bill 1943-44. It makes fascinating reading, well-documented with no less than 84 footnotes and cross-references in an article of 18 pages. Nevertheless, it is very readable, drawing deeply on the education papers in the Public Record Office, though curiously not seeming to use Butler's own autobiography, called remarkably enough *The Art of the Possible*. Politics, he claims, is the art of the possible and it is all he has attempted to achieve.

Looking back over the past fifty years, I find it difficult to assess how far educational theory has affected the course of politics, and how far political theory and practice have affected the almost constantly changing process of legislation and regulation in the field of education. I cannot recall any period in that half-century when we have not been engaged in quite radical educational reorganisation or – in that still more dangerous word – rationalisation. I have served in three dioceses, in one of which we actually had three different systems of educational legislation (mainland England, Jersey and Guernsey). We have had one Education Act after another. Yet in 1945 it was 'Rab's thing' – and he had done it.

Butler had of course served earlier at the Foreign Office under Halifax and Eden. It was in the summer of 1941 that he was given what he called 'my opportunity to harness to the educational system the war-time urge for social reform and greater equality'. He confesses that this task was much to his liking. He has described his summons to Churchill, who told him that he wished him to leave his mark on the Board of Education. He would be independent, and would be able to shift evacuated children from one place to another. Then Churchill went on, 'I am too old now to think that you can improve people's natures. Everyone has to learn to defend himself. I should not object if you could introduce a note of patriotism into the schools. Tell the children that Wolfe won Quebec.' Butler responded that he would like to influence what was taught in schools but that this was always frowned upon. Churchill's reply was, 'Of course not by instruction or order but by suggestion'. The interview ended by the Prime Minister saying, 'Come and see me to discuss things - not details, but the broad lines.' Answerable therefore, but a clear mandate - 'Rab's thing'.

There was another factor emerging which had to be taken into consideration. In December 1940 there had appeared one of those now famous letters to *The Times* which were signed jointly by the Archbishops of Canterbury and York, Cardinal Hinsley and the Moderator of the Free Church Federal Council. Under the heading 'Foundations of Peace' - just months after Dunkirk and the threatened invasion of our island - they urged that extreme inequality of wealth and possessions be abolished; that every child, regardless of race or class, should have equal opportunities of education, suitable for development of his particular capacities; that the family unit should be safeguarded, and that a sense of divine vocation should be restored to man's daily work. (Exclusive language was not yet a problem.) In June 1941 the Board of Education published its *Green Book* to serve as a basis for discussion with all interested bodies. Butler admits that many of its proposals, notably those dealing with the problems of church schools, did not survive exposure, but he claims that its production 'did stimulate thinking about educational reform and inspired a spate of booklets on the subject, each in its own distinctive colour'.

To help him in his task of producing eventually a White Paper, Butler had not only a cluster of civil servants, but as a Parliamentary Secretary, Chuter Ede, Labour and a non-Conformist - a Unitarian, I believe - with a dour countenance which belied both his integrity and his sense of humour. Together they worked on proposals for elementary education to the age of 11, and secondary education for all over that age, providing training suited to the talents of every individual to be combined with more expert training for industry, and with a practical form of continued education. They went no further on the religious aspect, which had seen in recent years one proposal after another. They merely called for a final settlement of the dual system of provided and non-provided schools. They were anxious, so Butler claimed afterwards, to avoid the renewed cry of 'Rome on the rates'. In general terms the non-Conformists wanted the dual system abolished, but came together with the Anglicans in accepting the agreed syllabus of religious teaching. But Cardinal Hinsley, for the Roman Catholics, rejected it as 'disembodied Christianity'. In another letter to *The Times*, the old man wrote (alone this time) just months before he died: 'No equal opportunity will exist for a minority who are saddled with extra and crushing financial burdens because of their definite religious convictions and because they cannot accept a syllabus of religious instruction agreeable to many'. Churchill had that cut out of the newspaper and sent to Butler with a note saying, 'There, you are fixed.'

I could take the rest of Holy Week to give you an account of all that followed; perhaps you will read the various exchanges in *Recusant History*. In brief, the voluntary bodies were offered two possibilities. Under the first they would receive a 100 percent grant towards the maintenance and repair of buildings (in addition to the payment of teachers' salaries) for which they would concede the appointment of teachers to the LEA, and accept an 'agreed syllabus' for religious education. The alternative would allow the voluntary bodies to retain the appointment of teachers and the teaching of their own religious syllabus, but the government grant in this case would be only 50 percent. Our bishops of that time felt in conscience unable to accept the first option and felt penalised for their religious beliefs in the second. So they pressed for a 100 percent grant, which was at once refused.

There were thereafter endless discussions and negotiations, not helped by the death of Cardinal Hinsley on St Patrick's Day 1943 (regarded by some as an act of English defiance of the liturgy, as it meant an annual requiem Mass in Westminster Cathedral that day, to the dismay of Irish visitors) and by the absence in Ireland through illness of Archbishop Downey, regarded by Butler as the leader of the Roman Catholic opposition. In his convalescence the Archbishop had mellowed and conceded that his objections were simply financial. Catholics were being asked to pay 50 percent of a huge but unknown sum. Butler undertook a clear estimate for the whole country of the cost to Catholics of the proposals in the White Paper, but there remained problems about redundant schools, new schools and compulsory power to acquire sites. Downey asked about the possibility of interest-free loans, but was warned off arousing non-Catholic opposition. It was even suggested that time was on his side. Once the heat was off, easements to remove legitimate hardships would prove possible. Though the financial burden seemed heavy, it could be spread over the years.

Archbishop Godfrey, as Apostolic Delegate, intervened to claim that the government was willing to pay 100 percent for atheists but not for Catholics who believed that education and religion were one and the same thing. Butler responded that the State could not be expected to take on the responsibility of paying fully for what he called 'the personal religion of any particular section of the community'. If the Church of England was prepared to accept the White Paper solution, why should he hold back from his scheme because of a contentious minority? Archbishop Williams of Birmingham pleaded for 75 percent, related to a provision in the 1936 Act, and discussion took place with one bishop after another. Eventually it was agreed that Butler and Ede should meet the northern bishops at their Ushaw fastness. Butler describes the encounter (*The Art of the Possible*, p. 106):

> *Near Durham we came to the imposing parterres of Ushaw College. We were greeted by the Bishop of Hexham, in full robes, and taken almost at once into the evening meal, which, in the tradition of the younger Pitt, was served at about 6 o'clock. There was a large gigot and tolerable quantities of a red wine. Immediately this feast was over we were taken to see the Chapel, and a magnificent ivory figure was taken down from the High Altar for our benefit. We were all filled with a certain awe, which was no doubt intentionally administered. Chuter Ede told me he thought he was going to faint.*

It seems that Butler and Ede returned to London, depressed at the prospects. However, some progress had been made. He records that Bishop Marshall of Salford 'desired his followers to suffer and pay as part of their faith. Flynn of Lancaster said that he could work the scheme. Downey told Chuter Ede and myself that it would enable him to get over all his troubles in Liverpool. But in the event, none of them attempted to control their own supporters.' What in fact had Butler offered? No more than an indication by a process of geometrical progression of the steady growth of aid to voluntary schools from 1870 onwards. If the bishops were patient and accepted the 50 percent settlement, they could hope for more within another generation.

In November that year, the Board gave the bishops a departmental estimate of the total Catholic liabilities for the country, amounting to just under ten million pounds. When just weeks later the Bill was introduced into parliament, the debates – according to Archbishop George Andrew Beck – were remarkably placid. It took just nineteen days to pass through parliament. On 5 January the hierarchy stated that it could never accept the Bill in its present form and the Bishop of Lancaster described its financial provisions as lunacy. But the voice of moderation was on the way. Archbishop Griffin was appointed to Westminster and installed there on 18 January. Butler himself describes the scene in the Commons next day as he was introducing the second reading of his Bill:

I had just got to the second part of my speech, in which I anticipated playing against the wind, when Mgr Griffin, the newly appointed Archbishop of Westminster who had been enthroned the day before, was ushered into the Distinguished Strangers' Gallery. There, with the sun illuminating his bright red hair and his pectoral cross, he sat looking directly down on me as I outlined the provision of the religious settlement and replied to those who had criticised its compromises: 'I would ask those who feel deeply,' I said, 'to dismiss from their minds the wholly unwarrantable views that the government desire either to tear away church schools from unwilling managers or to force them inhumanely out of business. The best way I can reassure them is by quoting a verse from the hymn: Ye fearful saints, fresh courage take, / The clouds ye so much dread / Are big with mercy, and shall break / In blessings on your head.'

The unexpected, gratifying and witty sequel was the delivery to me next morning of a large parcel, containing not a bomb but a set of Abbot Butler's Lives of the Saints, *the classic Roman Catholic work of hagiography. Indeed, I must in fairness say that, though the Roman Catholic interest never accepted the financial basis laid down for voluntary school building, the religious clauses aroused far less acrimony and a much greater sense of responsibility in the House of Commons than past experience had suggested was likely.*

Did the bishops never accept the financial basis laid down for voluntary school building, as Butler alleges? My own view is that under protest they did accept that the new provision should not be fought beyond the brink. Perhaps it would be better to lose this encounter and live to fight another day when a greater degree of justice might be obtained. I believe that the pleadings with the northern bishops at Ushaw achieved a pragmatic victory for the politicians. Griffin's victory was not to surrender but to achieve a united hierarchy, lest one diocese be played off against another by differing LEAs. He called all the bishops to Westminster for an extraordinary meeting at which the various alternatives were considered. He asked his secretaries to bring in a tray of drinks to the assembly in the Upper Library soon after midday. As they entered the room with their trays, the Archbishop called out to them, 'Wait just a minute, please, we are almost there.' They backed out of the room, and less than a minute later there was a burst of applause and the doors were opened from within. 'Drinks all round,' said the *Praeses Perpetuus*, and as the Private Secretary passed behind him he muttered, 'Unanimous, I think.'

The Butler Bill passed the Commons on 12 May 1944. One more attempt was made without avail in the Lords to cut the liability percentage, and the Royal Assent to the Bill was given on 3 August. Two years later amending legislation began. Then it was that Cardinal Griffin spoke out. He told how Butler and Chuter Ede had assured his brother bishops that

> *they understood our great difficulties. We should give the Act a fair trial. If we found it quite impossible to meet the requirements of the new Act we always had the remedy of an Amending Act. That remains true. There have in fact already been two Amending Acts, and on both occasions the Act has been amended in favour of the Ministry.*

Ladies and gentlemen, from that hypothetical ten million pounds you can carry on this story. At the time of which I have spoken we battled for the rights of parents. More recently and no more successfully in the Education Reform Act we have battled for the rights of trustees. Of his battle with Cardinal Hume, Kenneth Baker has written in *The Turbulent Years*: 'In the Anglican tradition I argued for the supremacy of parliament, for at the end of the day the issue was who should determine the law relating to the education of English children in England.'

Perhaps I should give the last word to my predecessor, Archbishop George Andrew Beck, writing in *The English Catholics* (1950):

In England and Wales today the Catholic schools are more than ever, then, missionary schools. In measurable time they may be the only ones left. Were they to be lost to the country, as God's Church sees it, all would be lost. Wherefore, by that dispensation with which Providence chastens its children, it was the task of the bishops in the last century to create these schools, but, in the next century, to preserve them from extinction.

It is a weighty charge we leave with you today.

Cardinal Cahal Daly (1997)
THE CHURCH'S MAGISTERIUM IN FACE
OF THE MORAL CRISIS OF OUR TIME

That there is moral crisis in our time few would deny. A wide range of behaviours which, until comparatively recently, would have been regarded as morally wrong by majority public opinion and would have been officially condemned as sinful by virtually all the Christian churches, and indeed by the great religious traditions of the world, are now widely regarded in public opinion as morally blameless and are indeed socially acceptable and in some cases legally sanctioned. There is no need to give examples, they are evident all around us, they exist in all social strata and pervade much of what we like to call 'the developed world'.

It is not only in practical behaviour that this moral change has come about; the actual moral principles and values by which people justify behaviour have themselves changed. The very concept of universally valid moral principles is today called in question, so that we can say that the moral values now commonly invoked make moral consensus in society virtually impossible, and indeed make it in principle impossible to call any behaviour morally wrong in any absolute or universal sense. The principle of universality has, however, been accepted by the main stream of western tradition over many centuries as the specific characteristic of moral discourse. From pre-Christian Rome, for example, we have the following declaration:

There is in fact a true law - namely right reason - which is in accordance with nature, applies to all men, and is unchangeable and eternal. By its commands this law summons men to the performance of their duties; by its prohibitions it restrains them from doing wrong. ... To invalidate this law by human legislation is never morally right, nor is it permissible ever to restrict its operation, and to annul it wholly is impossible. Neither the senate nor the people can absolve us from our obligations to obey this law, and it requires no (jurist) to expound and interpret it.

It will not lay down one rule at Rome and another at Athens, nor will it be one rule today and another tomorrow. But there will be one law, eternal and unchangeable, binding at all times upon all people; and there will be, as it were, one common master and ruler of men, namely God, who is the author of this law, its interpreter and its sponsor. The man who will not obey will abandon his better self, and, in denying the true nature of man, will thereby suffer the severest of penalties, though he has escaped all the other consequences which men call punishment.

This statement is from Marcus Tullius Cicero (*De Republica* III 33).

I pass to the beginning of the modern period, and to one of the leading thinkers of the 'Enlightenment', Immanuel Kant. Kant, as is well known, regarded the universality of moral principle as a defining quality of moral judgement, indeed as 'the type' of the moral law. Kant wrote: 'Act only on that maxim whereby thou canst at the same time will that (your maxim) should become universal law.' This is Kant's first formulation of the 'categorical imperative'. He goes on to give two other formulations. The second is: 'So act as to treat humanity, whether in thine own person or in that of any other, in every case as an end and never only as a means.' This is preceded by the statement that there is a being 'whose existence has in itself an absolute worth, something which, being an end in itself, could be a source of definite laws'. The human person is such a being, who 'exists as an end in himself, not merely as a means to be arbitrarily used' by others. The third formulation of the categorical imperative is 'the idea of the will of every rational being as a universal legislative will'.

The categorical imperative, in each of its three formulations, enables Kant to pronounce certain specific types of behaviour as objectively and universally and absolutely wrong: for example, suicide, promise-breaking, failure to respect the rights of others; all of these are held by him to contradict the very nature of moral law and, to be, therefore, intrinsically morally wrong. Furthermore, the human race is called and indeed obliged to aim at becoming a 'kingdom of ends', namely 'a union of different rational beings in a system of common laws'. This latter comes close to a statement of the rationality and objectivity and universality of human rights, where every person is, as an end in himself or herself, morally entitled to be treated as such by others and is, reciprocally, morally obliged to treat others as each an end in themselves and never as a means to some else's end.

Kant's *Critique of Practical Reason* therefore, has many of the elements of the great Graeco-Roman and Judaeo-Christian moral tradition which is the basis of western civilisation, even if Kant's formulation paradoxically carried within it the seeds of a philosophical overgrowth which later seriously damaged that tradition. The contemporary situation is in effect a reversal of both the Graeco-Roman and the Judaeo-Christian and of the Kantian insistence on the objectivity, the immutability and the universal validity of moral principles and, consequently, of human rights.

Crisis of civilisation

The rejection by many, both in principle and in practice, of these moral principles, therefore, amounts to a real moral crisis, a crisis of culture, of immense magnitude and of potentially very serious implications for the future of humanity. Indeed this has to be called a crisis of civilisation; for it contains many of the elements of an abandonment in principle of the concept of natural law, which has been a foundation principle of western civilisation since Graeco-Roman times, and which still underlays both the French and the

American revolutions, and which, to this day, underpins the efforts within the United Nations to obtain international recognition and eventual enforcement of a universal charter of human rights, based on moral duties which are universal in time and in place, and from which no state and no individual can claim exemption.

This is the moral consensus on which freedom under truth and freedom under law depend, and consequently on which the future of civilisation depends. But this consensus is fatally undermined by the growing acceptance in our culture of moral relativism or moral subjectivism, and by the acceptance in too many sectors of Catholic moral theology of a theory of consequentialism or proportionalism, which bases moral judgement on a subjective calculation of the overall consequences of an action, rather than on its intrinsic and objective moral nature.

Conscience

I wish to look at one or two of the frightening lessons to be learned from the crisis. One lesson is that of the fragility of the moral conscience. Conscience is indeed, as the Second Vatican Council says, 'the most secret core and sanctuary of man', where he is 'alone with God, whose voice echoes in his depths' (*Gaudium et Spes*, n. 16). But, as Newman pointed out, the noble name of conscience can be debased into 'a liberty of self-will'. 'What', Newman asked a century and a quarter ago, 'if a man's conscience embraces the idea of ... infanticide or free love?' This would, for Newman, be 'of all conceivable absurdities the wildest and most stupid'. Yet we are all too sadly aware how widespread, in contemporary society, even among Catholics, is, precisely, 'free love'; sexual intercourse before marriage, cohabitation, relations outside marriage, have become commonplace. Indeed, infanticide itself will sometimes be condoned in media and public debate on grounds of compassion for a distressed mother; while 'partial birth' abortions, which are impossible to distinguish from infanticide, are camouflaged as a necessary part of 'reproductive health care', and are presently in danger of being explicitly legally sanctioned in the United States of America; and abortion, which is morally of the same genus as infanticide, has become common obstetric practice in most of the countries of Europe and North America.

The virtually universal moral consensus about the evil of abortion, which prevailed until comparatively recently, has been superseded with remarkable speed in many countries by a social and cultural and legal acceptance of abortion, to the point where 'walk-in' abortions can calmly be advertised as a service to women's health. Sterilisation, which once was regarded with horror and was associated with the moral depravity and wickedness of Nazism, is now commonly presented as merely a simple and normal surgical procedure, and has even been hailed as 'the most loving thing a man can do for a woman'.

Nor is this debasing of conscience and of language found only in the realms of sex and reproduction; it is found also in politics, in business and finance, in the arms trade, in the practices of terrorism and in the conduct of war and the growing prevalence of crime accompanied by violence. In many of these areas, we find a casual acceptance of such principles as that 'the end justifies the means', 'it increases profits', 'it increases employment', etc. How much more shamefully true it is, therefore, in contemporary society than it was when Newman wrote his *Letter to the Duke of Norfolk*, that,

> *In this age, with a large portion of the public (conscience) is the very right and freedom of conscience to dispense with conscience, to ignore a lawgiver and judge. ... Conscience is a stern monitor, but, in this century, it has been superseded by a counterfeit, which the eighteen centuries prior to it never heard of and could not have mistaken for it if they had. It is the right of self-will.*

The speed and apparent ease with which conscience itself can be conditioned and corrupted raises very serious pastoral questions for the Church in a pluralist society.

Power of words

A second lesson of the contemporary moral and cultural crisis is that of the power of words to alter moral perceptions and to persuade people that what once was sin is now morally licit. We need not look far for examples. It has become 'politically incorrect' to use moral language about behaviour, because this is 'judgemental' and 'discriminatory', and causes 'unhealthy guilt feelings' in others. Moral judgement is often casually assumed to be a private matter for oneself only; and no individual is allowed any right to judge others by his or her private moral standards, or to impose her or his moral values on others. Instead, people have come to use morally neutral terms, or terms of psychological categorisation or socio-medical classification, or even terms of commendation of the agent, but very rarely moral condemnation of another's actions.

Thus the word 'fornication' is banished from public discourse and is replaced by such terms as 'being in a relationship', divorce is 'a second relationship', adultery is 'having an affair', contraception or even sterilisation is 'responsible sex'. In other areas of behaviour, we speak of civilian casualties in war as 'collateral damage', of area bombing as 'precision bombing', of low-wage economies as 'tiger economies' or as economies which 'follow the laws of the marketplace'. Deliberately ending the life of a senile or incurably ill person is called 'letting him or her die with dignity'. The abuse of language in these cases is manifest. Pope John Paul, in *Evangelium Vitae*, has referred in this connection to St Paul's description of pagan Rome as composed of people who 'become futile in their thinking', whose 'senseless minds are darkened' (n. 24).

Power of language

A further abuse of language which is relevant to the present moral debate is the use of words, not to communicate about a moral issue, but to discredit the opponent and disqualify him or her from being even listened to. In recent debates in Ireland about abortion and about divorce, for example, no terms were more often used in the media and in public discussion about pro-life and anti-divorce spokespersons or groups than terms like 'fundamentalists', 'extremists', or - horror of horrors - 'extremist fundamentalists', or 'right-wing Catholics', 'conservative Catholics', 'old-style Catholics', 'sectarian bigots'. The issues as such are not debated, but the protagonists for life and for family are labelled in such a way as to exclude them from 'modern', 'progressive' and 'civilised' society and consequently to classify them as people whose views could by definition have no validity. We know how often the teaching of Pope John Paul is similarly dismissed by derogatory remarks about his so-called 'conservative' background in 'pre-Vatican II Polish Catholicism', or about his alleged attempts to 'roll back' the Vatican Council, *et cetera*.

The persuasive power of ethical terms, which Charles L Stevenson developed into a comprehensive theory of ethics, has certainly played a part in today's moral crisis. Ian Robinson, in a book on *The Survival of English*, has spoken of 'linguistic magic'. Pope John Paul again calls attention to this seductive danger and urges us, 'now more than ever to have the courage to look the truth in the eye and to call things by their proper names without yielding to convenient compromises or to the temptation of self-deception. ... No words have the power to change the intrinsic reality of things' (*Evangelium Vitae*, n. 58).

Religion and morality

Another conclusion to be drawn from the contemporary crisis is that religious faith and morality are very closely connected. It has long been a dogma of secular humanists that ethics is completely independent of religion and carries within itself its own self-validating power. Indeed, following Kant, many, if not most, moral philosophers have held that decisions and choices made for religious motives are not truly moral; it is said that moral choices have to be 'autonomous', whereas choices made on religious grounds are 'heteronomous', and therefore morally inauthentic. Surely, however, it would be implausible to deny that the crisis in contemporary morals has been, not just accompanied by, but in large part caused by, decline in religious faith and practice. Pope John Paul is surely right when he calls, in both of his great moral encyclicals, for a deep conversion of consciences and an individual and collective response to the Christian call to contemplative prayer and to holiness. Nothing less will equip us to resist the modern 'culture of death' and to create a new 'culture of life'.

The decline in moral thinking and in moral standards in contemporary society, however, does not justify a blanket condemnation of modern society, and does not make critics of this decline into nostalgic, backward-looking, *laudatores temporis acti*. There was immorality in every society throughout history, and there is much in modern society which represents genuine moral progress. We must as Christians embrace all that is true and good in modern culture; and indeed it is those who have a deep understanding and a genuine appreciation of what is true and good in modern society who can most credibly criticise what is erroneous and evil. This is precisely how Pope John Paul views modern culture, with full appreciation of 'the positive signs at work in humanity's present situation'. He warns against 'sterile discouragement', and enumerates many 'signs of hope' which give us courage (*Evangelium Vitae*, nn. 26-27).

Role of magisterium

The modern crisis of morality unfortunately coincided with something of a crisis in Catholic moral theology. The profound renewal of dogmatic theology which climaxed in the Second Vatican Council was preceded by many decades of previous preparation. A number of distinguished Catholic exegetes and theologians were laying the foundations long before the Council, particularly in the post-World War II period. Great names like those of Bea, Benoît, Feuillet, Dupont in scripture, and von Balthasar, Rahner, de Lubac and Congar in theology, come immediately to mind. Sadly, there were no comparable great names in moral theology, although Pope Pius XII had made very significant contributions to Catholic teaching on the great moral issues of his time. The Council itself did not formally address the area of moral theology, although its documents, especially *Gaudium et Spes*, have important paragraphs on moral themes, especially in the areas of marriage and family and social justice. The Council did, however, issue a call to scholars to undertake a renewal of moral theology, based on the teaching of scripture and responding to the problems and aspirations of modern culture (*Optatam Totius*, n. 16, and *Gaudium et Spes*, n. 62). Bernard Häring made a valiant effort to outline a new approach to moral theology, based on Christ's new commandment of love, but faithful to the great tradition of the Church. Unfortunately, however, like many others, Häring got caught up in the *Humanae Vitae* controversy and increasingly took the line of dissent.

The negative reaction of some to *Humanae Vitae* both exposed the existing weaknesses in the teaching of modern theology and created new weaknesses. Those in the first wave of dissent seemed sincerely to believe that the Church's traditional ruling on contraception could be changed without any effect on the rest of Catholic moral teaching. They quickly found, however, that the logic of their position on contraception went very much further than they had originally intended; indeed it obliged them to adopt positions which unravelled the whole of the Church's sexual morality, and, not only that, but also involved a drastic rewriting of large areas of traditional

Catholic moral teaching. Helped by an enthusiastically compliant media, dissent spread rather widely among the Catholic moral theological community and spread from there to considerable sections of the wider Catholic family. This undoubtedly weakened the Church's stand in face of the many grave evils confronting her in modern society. It was this situation that Pope John Paul II was addressing in his two great encyclicals, *Veritatis Splendor* in 1993 and *Evangelium Vitae* in 1995. In *Veritatis Splendor* Pope John Paul, in firm language, declares that (n. 29):

> *Within the context of the theological debates which have followed the Council there have developed certain interpretations of Christian morality which are not consistent with 'sound teaching'. ... The magisterium has the duty to state that some trends of theological thinking and certain philosophical affirmations are incompatible with revealed truth.*

The Pope makes it plain that conscience is not the source of values (n. 32). He strongly emphasised the truth that there are moral laws which bind universally and there are behaviours which are objectively and intrinsically evil in themselves (nn. 51-53). Three times in *Evangelium Vitae* Pope John Paul invokes holy scripture and the tradition of the Church and the universal magisterium of the bishops united with the Pope and his own Petrine authority, as well as the natural law, to declare specific acts to be intrinsically morally wrong (nn. 62, 65, 66):

> *By the authority which Christ conferred upon Peter and his successors, in communion with the bishops ... I declare that direct abortion, that is to say abortion willed as an end or as a means, always constitutes a grave moral disorder, since it is the deliberate killing of an innocent human being. ...*

I confirm that euthanasia is a grave violation of the law of God, since it is the deliberate and morally unacceptable killing of a human person. ...

Suicide is always as morally objectionable as murder. The Church's tradition has always rejected it as a gravely evil choice. ... Suicide, viewed objectively, is always a gravely immoral act.

Veritatis Splendor is addressed directly to bishops. The Pope speaks to them as 'brothers who share with me the responsibility of safeguarding sound teaching'. He speaks of himself and the bishops together as 'we pastors'. Obviously, this document is intended as a statement of the moral principles upheld by the Church's ordinary and universal magisterium. Published in 1995, *Evangelium Vitae* was prepared for by an especially convened consistory of cardinals in 1991, and by a questionnaire sent to every bishop in the Church. This encyclical is also, therefore, clearly an exercise of the ordinary and universal magisterium. Taken together, these two documents laid down firm principles for Catholic moral teaching and clear parameters for the still awaited renewal of Catholic moral theology.

Challenge to Church and society

These documents also constitute a challenge to Church and to society. The Pope is, as always, conscious that the Church is engaged in a mighty spiritual combat, and that only a real struggle for holiness of life on the part of all Catholics will arm us for that combat. He calls for a renewal of the sense of mystery, of wonder and of reverence before God and before God's gift of human life. He calls for the fostering of a contemplative outlook (*Evangelium Vitae*, n. 83), and a renewed sense of the sacredness of human life. He outlines what can be called a comprehensive and consistent pro-life ethic, indeed for a 'culture of life' to confront the growing 'culture of death' in modern society. He asks all Catholics to become 'people of life', so that, 'a new

117

culture of love and solidarity may develop for the true good of the whole of human society' (n. 101). The pressures against the Church's teaching in virtually all areas of morality might seem irresistible. A remark attributed to the American judge, Mr Justice Brandeis, is worth recalling: 'The irresistible is often only that which is not resisted' (cited by Isaiah Berlin, *Historical Inevitability*, 1953).

I wish to quote some remarkable words from a most unlikely witness, Bertrand Russell. In his notorious *Marriage and Morals*, Russell accurately foresaw, as many Catholic moral theologians did not foresee, that the introduction of contraception implied what he called an entirely new ethics of sexuality. In *The Scientific Attitude* (1931, 1954) he outlines some of the probable outcomes of the application of science to human problems, including the question of sex and reproduction. His predictions at the time had the character of science fiction, but they are now everyday matters of fact. He granted that his predictions were 'not to be taken altogether as serious prophecy'; they are 'visions of Cassandra'. Russell himself was clearly disturbed by these possibilities; he saw them as possibilities 'in a world governed by knowledge without love, and power without delight'. He deplores the cult of 'power for its own sake'; he fears those for whom, 'the fact that they can do something that no-one previously thought it possible to do is a sufficient reason for doing it'. They represent, he says, the world 'which would result if scientific technique were to rule unchecked'. Russell sees, though without much hope, possible alternatives in a rediscovery of contemplation. He speaks of 'the ecstasy of contemplation'. He quotes: 'In knowledge of God standeth our eternal life'. Sadly, for Russell ecstasy can come only from human love, chiefly sexual love; and this does not provide the 'peace that passes all understanding' which the human heart seeks, and which only God can give.

Pope John Paul, contemplative as well as pastor and teacher, brings us back in the end of *Evangelium Vitae* to Christ, who alone has the words of eternal life and to Mary, who kept all his words and pondered them in her heart. It is here that we find courage for the immense tasks which confront us as Catholics facing the moral crisis of our time. Like St Paul (*2 Corinthians* 4:8-9,18),

> *we are in difficulties on all sides, but never cornered; we see no answer to our problems, but never despair; we have been persecuted but never deserted; knocked down but never killed. ... So we have no eyes for things that are visible, but only for the things that are invisible; for visible things last only for a time, and the invisible things are eternal.*

Reflections in Holocaust Museum

While in Washington last month for a lecture, I visited the United States Holocaust Memorial Museum there. I am still haunted by the awful images of the 'culture of death' which surround one as one goes from gallery to gallery of that museum. The question that kept coming to me was this: 'How could this happen in a modern, advanced, technologically highly developed European country in the middle of the twentieth century? How could so many of the professional elites in such a country have tolerated this or even colluded in it? Could it happen here?' Our instinct is to reply immediately, 'impossible, unthinkable'; but we need to pause and reflect. When sterilisation, euthanasia, the elimination of the mentally or physically handicapped and of eugenically inferior breeds were introduced by the Nazis in 1935, shock waves of moral revulsion spread across the western world. Moral sensitivities have profoundly changed since then. There is no universal moral revulsion now when euthanasia, sterilisation, abortion, eugenic 'breeding', are discussed.

Professor Leibbrand, expert witness for the prosecution at the Nuremberg Trial of German doctors who conducted experiments on human beings in the Nazi regime, declared that the Nazis substituted the 'biological idea' for the 'metaphysical idea', and that it was this that mentally conditioned doctors for their systematic medical experimentation on human beings, particularly prisoners, internees and others. There are disturbing signs of a similar substitution of the biological view of the human being for the metaphysical view, and much more for the Christian view, in some medical circles today. The proposed re-writing of the Hippocratic Oath would scarcely have been possible without such a shift of meanings and of values. The inscription on a pillar in the chapel area in the Holocaust Museum reads: 'For the dead and the living we must bear witness'. Much more must we bear witness to the Lord of life, who came and dwelt amongst us in order that we might have life and might have it to the full.

Cardinal Basil Hume OSB (1998)
JESUS CHRIST TODAY

I was in Rome on 2 February 1983 when Father Henri de Lubac was made a cardinal. He was then eighty-seven years old. After receiving their birettas from the Pope the new cardinals go to those cardinals present to give and receive the kiss of peace. I never thought that I would be in that situation with a man who was one of the greatest theologians of this century. It was a humbling experience. Your invitation to deliver this lecture today in his memory recalls for me that moment, and I thank you for it.

I have been given the title 'Jesus Christ today' as the subject for this talk. To do justice to so noble a subject would require the skill and knowledge either of a great scholar or of a saint. Your speaker today is neither the one nor the other. He is a pastor preoccupied with guiding the flock for which he is responsible as best he can. The subject given would lead him to adopt the style more appropriate to the pulpit than to the lecture hall. I am not sure that this would be correct here. Nor would it be right to pretend to have kept up with all the study pursued by biblical scholars and others to discover the truth about the 'historical Jesus', for example.

So, how should I proceed? The phrase 'a spiritual odyssey' occurred to me as a possible subtitle to 'Jesus Christ today'. That sounds just a little too pompous. So where do I go now? I was once told that in communicating with others a little vulgar self-exposure was not only in order, but rather desirable. That went against every novice master's instruction to his novices. It is true that very often people want to discover not so much what you know, but what it means to you. They want to know how another came to believe, and just as importantly, why that person still believes to this day. 'Tell us your story,' they say, 'It will be more interesting than a lecture worked out and drawn up from learned tomes, and less irritating than a series of exhortations from a preacher.'

So, I shall tell you my story. I do so shyly, I confess, but I trust with sufficient diffidence not to irritate you. It explains how I have discovered just how important Jesus Christ is to me today, and will become, I trust, even more important tomorrow. It may take some time to get to the point where we shall meet Jesus Christ in my text. I am going to tell you about my pilgrimage through life as I have gone in search of God. Did I hear a voice crying 'objection'? What is your objection? 'Surely you were brought up a Catholic, went to a Catholic school, could boast how well you knew the catechism, went regularly to church?' Yes, indeed, all that is true, of course. But it is one thing to observe all the 'externals' of religion, to be able to hold one's own in an argument about religion, but quite another for it to be a matter which engages mind and heart, becomes an inspiration and guide for one's life. The child's belief must become the faith of the adult. If that does not happen we remain spiritually children, or, even worse, drop the whole thing. Every person, and this must include, of course, every Christian, has to find good reason to move into that experience of faith, which takes him or her into a realm of knowledge which goes beyond what is known through the five senses, or here scientific enquiry and experimentation are of no avail.

Let me explain how I first came to tell my story. I had been invited to speak to a captive audience of adolescents on the subject of 'God'. I was not certain as to which constituted the greater difficulty, the subject or the adolescents. I tried to look back to the time when I was their age, and see what had struck me then that remained important for me today. There were five experiences which, looking back, stood out. Of course, I now understand and speak about these experiences with the sophistication of the adult. Indeed, I have reflected and spoken about these experiences more than once, and in doing so I am aware that the language of the adult masks the crude impressions made by them on the adolescent mind.

The first experience I recall involved a coffin. One of my earliest childhood memories is the sight of a coffin being borne through the streets of Newcastle to its final resting place. I can still picture the scene. My thoughts at the time were no doubt childish and unformed, but the incident was a starting point which, over the years, led to more mature reflection and speculation. Why should death happen? Is it the end of everything, or could it be a new beginning? I found that I was unable to believe that death should be the end, the final irreversible act. It just did not seem right. Death seemed to make a mockery of human endeavours; the apparent finality of it, and its arbitrariness, seemed to trivialise and toss aside all human efforts and striving. Death could only make sense as the prelude to a richer, more lasting existence. The deepest promptings of the human spirit whisper that there is more to human life than the span of years allotted to it, and I began to search for something belonging to a different order of reality which would correspond to this deep intuition that death could not have the last word.

The second experience was the writing of an essay. When I was preparing for university entrance examinations at school it was the custom in those days in some subjects to be required to write a two or three hour essay on a single subject, often just one word. As you will imagine, the more abstract the word, the harder the task. The word we were given, which was to become a starting point in my search for God, was 'happiness'. I imagine that I had never really thought seriously about it before, and no doubt what I wrote reflected the first attempts at thinking by a seventeen year-old. What is happiness? Are people generally happy? Why are we happy at one moment and not at another? Happiness struck me then as elusive, eagerly desired, but impossible to grasp. Much later, I found in St Thomas Aquinas a teacher to guide me in this, as in much else.

Following Aristotle he argued that we were indeed made for happiness, but the kind of happiness we deeply crave must have two qualities if it is to be satisfying: it must be complete, leaving us with no other desires, and it must be permanent.

Experiences of happiness in our human condition, however, are essentially incomplete. We remain forever restless, now seeking this, now that. George Herbert understood well the part which restlessness can play in leading a person to God, and in the poem *The Pulley God* explains why, of all his gifts, he had withheld from man the gift of 'rest':

> *'For if I should', said he,*
> *'Bestow this jewel also on my creature,*
> *he would adore my gifts instead of me,*
> *And rest in Nature, not the God of Nature:*
> *so both should losers be.*
> *'Yet let him keep the rest,*
> *But keep them with repining restlessness,*
> *Let him be rich and weary, that at least,*
> *If goodness lead him not, yet weariness*
> *May toss him to my breast.'*

Something deep inside the human breast is never satisfied in this life, and if we are not ultimately to be frustrated, then it is elsewhere and in some other form of existence that we shall find a happiness, complete and without end.

The third experience I would like to speak about is very personal, but at the same time is shared by us all. It is the experience of love. It is exhilarating to discover another who will captivate our heart and occupy the empty space within it. It is thrilling to realise that we have a privileged place in someone else's heart and life. There is no need to elaborate on that experience. We discover that love can raise us to the heights, and also plunge us to the depths of despair. We find that human love can be fickle. But in my teens I began to learn that in some way we are made for love, and that all true human love, however transient and imperfect, has in it something of the infinite and eternal.

One of the most moving accounts of human love I have ever read is given by Viktor Frankl, who was imprisoned at Auschwitz. His wife was also a prisoner at a neighbouring camp, but they were not able to see each other. He writes of a moment in his own life at that terrible place. He was stumbling to work in the icy wind before dawn, one of the detachment of slaves, driven by guards using rifle butts. Suddenly his wife entered his mind.

Real or not, her look was then more luminous than the sun which was beginning to rise. A thought transfixed me, for the first time in my life I saw the truth as it is set into song by so many poets, proclaimed as the final wisdom by so many thinkers; that love is the ultimate and the highest goal to which man can aspire. I grasped the meaning of the greatest secret that human poetry and human thought and belief have to impart: the salvation of man is through love and in love.

I understood how a man who has nothing left in the world may still know bliss. ... In utter desolation, when man cannot express himself in positive action, when his only achievement may consist in enduring his sufferings in the right way, man can achieve fulfilment. For the first time in my life I was able to understand the meaning of the words, 'The angels are lost in perpetual contemplation of an infinite glory'.

(Viktor Frankl, *Observer Magazine*, 21 June 1992)

'The salvation of man is through love and in love' – few thoughts are more exhilarating than the realisation that 'God is love,' and has for each person an intensity of love which no human experience of love can match. That human experience is nonetheless a wonderful instrument whereby we may begin to explore the meaning of love in God. The 'ultimate and highest good', open to us all, is to be involved in that dialogue of love about which the saints and mystics have written.

These three boyhood experiences – thoughts about death, the desire for happiness, the reality of love – began to shape in me a simple philosophy of life. It was that I have no abiding city in this world; that I want and need to be happy; that happiness seems to consist in loving and being loved. None of these experiences proved in any sort of conclusive manner that God existed, yet each one was, and remains, a pointer to another form of life that would persist after death. Each experience carried within it glimpses and a promise of an existence characterised by an unending now of ecstatic joy when united to one who is, of all that is loveable, the most loveable of all.

A fourth experience was in my case a good example of passing from notional to real assent, as this process was understood by Cardinal Newman. I had known from studying philosophy the argument for the existence of God from contingency. Philosophers use the word 'contingent' to indicate that radical dependence of one being on another. Nothing in our experience is self-explanatory or totally self-sufficient. We live in a world of 'dependencies'. That world remains ultimately unexplained unless there exists a being which is totally self-sufficient and in no way in need of another, that is a being that is not contingent but necessary. It was only later that I came to understand what contingency meant, and was able to give real assent to the argument.

It is extremely important that religious belief should be seen to be, as I believe it is, intellectually credible. But belief is not forced upon our reason. The argument for God's existence from contingency was for me both attractive and personally conclusive, and yet it is not so overwhelming as to compel assent from everyone. It was when turning over these thoughts in my mind that I came across a quotation from Georges Bracque printed on the flyleaf of George Steiner's book, *Real Presences*. I read: '*Les preuves fatiguent la vérité*'. How does one translate that? Proofs, or arguments, obscure the truth. Or perhaps: proofs can make truth tedious. When I read that word from Bracque, I was driven to reflect on how truth can be discovered by intuition rather than established by reasoned argument. For my purposes this is important. Intuition is that knowledge of an object or that immediate assent to a truth which does not depend on the laborious process of logical reasoning. It is instead the impact made by an object or truth on the intellect. It is the sudden and immediate recognition by the mind of something, or indeed someone, other than itself. I liken it sometimes to the appearance of the objects in a room when the light is turned on. They were there in all their reality in the dark. The eye recognises what is there when the light appears. Objects are immediately recognised for what they are. At once, some of their qualities become evident without the need for demonstration or argumentation. Perhaps intuition is simply the turning on of a light, the lifting of a veil or the opening of a door to enable the human spirit to enter and possess its proper domain.

This leads me to the last of the five experiences I would like to describe. This was my personal discovery, through the poetry of Wordsworth, of the role of beauty as a way of contemplating God. I was still at school. The syllabus required, in addition to the main subjects in the Higher Certificate Examination, two additional subsidiary subjects. One of these covered some aspects of English literature. It was fashionable then in the Sixth Form for the cleverer boys to read and enjoy T S Eliot. It was less fashionable to admit to enjoying Wordsworth. I did. Discovery that he was able to sense the presence of God in nature quite transformed my attitude to all created beings. In *Lines Composed a Few Miles Above Tintern Abbey (13*

July 1798), Wordsworth described in enthralling terms his realisation that nature could disclose the presence of God:

> *And I have felt*
> *A presence that disturbs me with the joy*
> *Of elevated thoughts; a sense sublime*
> *Of something far more deeply interfused,*
> *Whose dwelling is the light of setting suns,*
> *And the round ocean and the living air,*
> *And the blue sky, and in the mind of man:*
> *A motion and a spirit, that impels*
> *All thinking things, all objects of all thought,*
> *And rolls through all things.*

I realised, at first only dimly no doubt, that God was not, of course, part of his creation but that nonetheless all that exists not only owes its origin to him, but in some manner also reflects him just as a work of art speaks of the artist who created it. Thus in all that is good and beautiful some glimpse is given of those qualities in God – in a manner which is of course different but, as the theologians tell us, is analogous. We are given some idea of his glory, a hint only, but precious indeed.

Such experiences as I have described are like shafts of light breaking through that cloud that separates us from the vision of God. They lighten up the way for the pilgrim and warm his heart, but they do not suffice. I need – and increasingly – one who will come to me and tell me about God. If only one would come, a pilgrim coming from the opposite direction, who would explain how to reach the end of the journey, and who knows what lies beyond the here and now. I think I recognise him as the one about whom I learned as a child, about whom teachers used to speak, and priests from the pulpit. He was an acquaintance only, if the truth be told. I knew all the answers to the questions these put to me about him, but him I did not know - not really. Then one day, sitting by the wayside on my pilgrim way, disconsolate, confused, uncertain - though a seemingly brash self-confidence masked that reality - I heard him say: 'I am the way, the truth and the life, no one comes to the Father, but by me' (*John* 14:6).

Then he put three questions to me. He spoke and said: 'Who do you say that I am?' Was not that the question he had once asked Peter? How magnificently Peter had answered: 'You are the Christ, the Son of the living God.' How had Peter known? How was it that he was able to express this belief so clearly, so categorically? 'Flesh and blood has not revealed this to you, but my Father who is in heaven' (*Matthew* 16:15-17). That question is being put to you and me today: 'Who do you say that I am?' It is faith that takes us where our senses cannot go. It is one thing to research the origins of the Gospels, test their historical authenticity, and consult near-contemporary authors. It is quite another to be able to acknowledge the reality to which Peter confessed. He saw one thing, a man; he believed another, that this man was God too. Any attempt to belittle this truth, either by exaggerating the divinity at the expense of the humanity, or by emphasising the humanity at the expense of the divinity, is wrong.

I had a point to make to the pilgrim who had come to meet me. 'Show me the Father', I said, 'and I shall be satisfied. Tell me what God is like. I want to know.' That had been Philip's prayer: 'Have I been with you so long, and yet you do not know me, Philip? He who has seen me has seen the Father' (*John* 14:8-9). 'No one knows the Father except the Son and anyone whom the Father chooses to reveal him' (*Matthew* 11:27). Philip's words echo a prayer spoken by Moses: 'Show me your glory' (*Exodus* 33:18). But that was not possible: 'my face you cannot see, for no human being can see me and survive'. Moses was told by God to hide in the cleft of a rock; he would be shielded by the hand of God when God was to pass by. 'Then I shall take my hand away and you will see my back.' In other words Moses would see something of God, but not God himself. We cannot see God as he is.

Over the years we try as best we can to create for ourselves an idea or an image of what God might be like. George Tyrell, a theologian at the end of the last century, commented quite pertinently on that effort (*External Religion: its use and abuse*):

> *God is not directly reached by our mind, or our imagination, but only an idea or picture of God, which we ourselves have constructed out of the fragments of our experience. Those 'fragments' are a crude, childish representation at the best. It is not God, but only that crude image of God we set before our mind's eye when we pray to him or think of him, and try to love him, and find it so hard to succeed. No wonder, then, that he seems so far away, so uncertain, so intangible.*

Nonetheless, I believe that in all that is true, good and beautiful we can get a glimpse of God, a fleeting glance, not, of course, the vision of him. That is for later on. Nor, indeed, can Christ himself show us in our present state God as he really is. Nonetheless, Christ came to tell us about the Father. As man he translates for us into human terms the truth about God, to enable us to understand, in so far as we can, something of him.

God is in Christ because Christ is God. Thus every word that he spoke and everything that he did put us in touch with God through Christ's humanity. The consequences of these are momentous, and I choose that word advisedly. What we cannot discover about God on our own, unaided, we can learn from the study of Jesus Christ in the Gospels. The Gospels are not, then, just records of what Christ said and did, but they enable us to listen to his voice speaking to us now and to study the manner of his acting in our regard. Theologians use the word 'theandric' to describe the actions of Christ. They are the actions of God who became man. He spoke human words and acted in a human manner, but the person so speaking and acting was God. Although the words he spoke and his actions occurred at a particular moment in time, they have, nonetheless, a timeless quality about them, making them relevant in every age, and personal to every person. That is why the Gospels are central to the life of the Church and to the prayer life of each individual as well.

In the fifteenth chapter of St Luke's Gospel there are three parables – about a lost sheep, a woman searching for a lost coin, and a prodigal son. We learn, in a very remarkable manner, something vitally important for us about God in these parables. You will recall the story of the lost sheep. Seen through our eyes, we might label the shepherd's actions as irresponsible. To ignore and leave a sizeable flock of sheep 'in the wilderness', and go and look for one sheep seems strange behaviour. We might even be tempted to advise the shepherd to 'cut his losses'. After all, what is one sheep among so many? But that is through our eyes, and we forget Jesus is actually talking to us about God. The glimpse of God he offers is breathtaking. It is the God for whom one among so many does count; it is the God who will look out for us; it is the God who will rejoice when he finds us.

Today's sophisticated minds find it hard to believe that God became man, that he died on the cross, and then rose again from the dead. These truths and much else in our Christian faith are often ignored in our contemporary culture. We have grown out of religion. We are now adult. Are we? I wonder. Can we not be humble enough to acknowledge that there could be a reality which we could not discover for ourselves? We need to recapture a sense of mystery.

A mystery is a truth that lies beyond us. It is too rich for our understanding. It can be entered into, explored, inhabited even; but it can never be exhausted or fathomed. Our age dislikes intensely the idea of mystery, because it directly exposes our limitations. The thought that there could be something – or someone – beyond human comprehension or imagining is of course exciting, but it is also belittling. It puts us in our place and that is not at the centre.

Science has played an important role here, at once dispelling apparent mysteries and solving problems, and continually pushing forward the boundaries of human knowledge. And its success, and especially the visible effects of technology, has led many to the very unscientific conclusion that what science can eventually discover and dissect is all there is to reality. The truth is that the whole scientific enterprise is itself an exploration of an ordered creation, but it is inherently a limited one. There is far more to life than science, and the picture of 'reality' which the physical and biological sciences provide is inevitably partial.

I and you are being asked another question by that pilgrim who came to join us. Caught in an unbelieving mood, scepticism and intellectual pride surfacing once again, the pilgrim asks me and you: 'Do you also wish to go away?' Peter, when he was asked, replied: 'Lord, to whom shall we go? You have the words of eternal life; and we have believed, and have come to know, that you are the holy one of God' (*John* 6:67-69). We believe not because we understand and see clearly the truths of our faith, but because we have been taught them by him who can neither deceive nor be deceived. These truths are revealed. We accept them and then spend a lifetime exploring them. Happily we have an authentic teacher in the Church who, with a special help from the Holy Spirit, can guide us not to deviate from the truth. The teacher is known by a Latin name, the *magisterium*.

This question of truth is, I believe, sometimes evaded. There is an attitude which says, 'Who can tell what is true? The only reason for being spiritual or going to church is if you find it helpful, if it makes you feel better.' But, of course, it matters crucially whether God in fact exists, and whether Jesus Christ is, in fact, his Son sent to redeem us. If it is not true, if the central and objective claims of Christianity are false, then we are deluded, worshipping a chimera.

On the other hand, if the claims of Christianity are true then this transforms everything. Whether it is helpful is entirely secondary. The key question is whether Christianity is true. And it cannot both be true and not matter. So the pilgrim's question – 'Do you wish to go away?' – focuses our attention on the foundation of our belief, and the revealed truth in which we put our trust.

There was a third question which Jesus asks: 'Do you love me?' That was indeed a remarkable question, and especially when, on asking Peter a third time, Jesus used a word that denoted warm and affectionate intimacy. You recall how Peter responded, and with just a note of exasperation in his voice, 'You know all things, you know that I love you' (*John* 21:15–17).

I believe that when Jesus said on the cross, 'I thirst', that he was expressing his deepest and strongest desire, namely to be part of the lives of each one of us. It was a human cry to echo the voice of divine love calling us to intimacy with the God who is the lover of each one of us. Does that frighten you? It astonishes me, but at the same time it is immensely consoling, indeed thrilling. If 'God is love', as St John tells us in his first letter, then there is none more loveable than God, and none his equal in the act of loving.

St Paul wrote in his letter to the Galatians: 'I have been crucified with Christ; it is no longer I who live, but Christ who lives in me, and the life I now live in the flesh I live by faith in the Son of God, who loved me and gave himself for me' (*Galatians* 2:20). Does this mean that Christ lives in St Paul's mind and in his heart, as friends and those whom you love tend to linger on in our thoughts and affections? That, certainly. Paul had heard words that even now, read by us, are very striking. Paul was on the road to Damascus: 'Saul, Saul, why do you persecute me? ... I am Jesus, whom you are persecuting'

(*Acts* 9:4,5). Christ lived in those whom Paul was persecuting, just as he lives in the hungry, the thirsty, the naked, as we learned from the last judgement scene told to us by St Matthew (*Matthew* 25). We have, I believe, entered (maybe 'trespassed' is a more appropriate word) into a reality which far exceeds our capacity to understand it. All I do know is that when I receive his body and blood in the Eucharist, he enters into me in a remarkable manner, and there, I trust, continues to abide so that in truth I can say, 'I live, now no longer I, but Christ lives in me'. Others, especially the mystics, would explain this better than I, but it is appropriate for us to speculate on the meaning of these strange, but vitally important 'sayings' of St Paul. Christ is within me where he has made his abode.

I have taken you on my pilgrim journey, and reflected with you on my continuing search for God, because the personal seeking of God, I believe, lies at the heart of religion. The spiritual quest is the soul of religion, and the source of its energy and vitality. And yet for many on that quest the institutional church is alien. They ask: 'Why should I go to church? Why can't I just worship my own God in my own way? Surely religion is about my personal relationship with God. Why do I need to bring other people into what is a private matter?' From earliest times, following Jesus was never just a private, personal matter. Christians came together to live in community, to profess their faith in Jesus Christ, true God and true man, to witness to his resurrection, and live by his teachings. The profound reason for this is given to us by Christ himself, when he said: 'I am the vine, you are the branches' (*John* 15:5).

We meet here once again a reality which defies the ability of the human mind either to discover or to understand fully. It is a mystery. The mystery is the precise nature of the relationship of Christ to the baptised, and of the baptised to each other. Just as the sap gives life to the vine, so the life of Christ gives life to all the baptised. The vine and its branches are one. There is mutual interdependence of branch and vine, and of branch with branch. St Paul's analogy of the head and the body explains the same relationship of the members to the head, and the mutual interdependence of the members to each other. St Paul wrote (*1 Corinthians* 12:14): 'there are many parts, yet one body. The eye cannot say to the hand, "I have no need of you", nor again the head to the feet, "I have no need of you".' We need each other. Those who claim that they have no need of others, should pause to consider the importance of contributing to the good of others. The foot does need the hand, though it may not be immediately self-evident. We are always in danger of being too self-regarding in our spiritual lives. It is not just what we get out of it that matters, but, more importantly, what we can contribute. To say, 'I will follow Jesus but not the Church', is to separate Jesus from the Church, to cut off the branches from the vine.

We are reflecting on the theme 'Jesus Christ today' as we are preparing for the celebration of the millennium. It is therefore a subject that has a particular relevance at the present time. There is no need for us, Christians, to tell each other why we are going to celebrate. We admit, of course, that two thousand years since the birth of Christ may be no more than an approximation to the actual date, but that is of little consequence. The dating is acknowledged to be '*anno Domini*'. So it is the fact that God become man and dwelt amongst us which is the reason for our celebration. We recognise this to be the central moment of history. The year 2000 cannot just be a continuous new year's party. Indeed, for non-Christians who do not accept Jesus Christ as God made man, the beginning of a new millennium should mark a new beginning for them too. We want the world to be a better place and, presumably, we would like to be better people. That must include, surely, the reawakening of that spiritual instinct which I believe to be within each person.

We read in St Luke's Gospel that shortly after beginning his public ministry Jesus returned to his home town, and went to the synagogue. He was handed the scroll and he read from the prophet *Isaiah* (61:1-2):

> *The Spirit of the Lord God is upon me, because the Lord has anointed me to bring good tidings to the afflicted: he has sent me to bind up the broken-hearted, to proclaim liberty to the captives, and the opening of the prison to those who are bound, to proclaim the year of the Lord's favour.*

Then Jesus sat down. All eyes in the synagogue were fixed on him. 'These words,' he said, 'are being fulfilled today even as you listen' (*Luke* 4:21). The messianic era, long foretold, had begun. The 'year of the Lord's favour' had arrived, and Christ carried in himself that 'favour from the Lord' which was essentially to be the good news.

If we are to make the millennium significant then this calls for a profound change of heart in each one of us. 'Repent, and believe the good news,' said Jesus. That personal change of heart must have its impact on society today. We live in a world in which, and to which, we are called to proclaim the year of the Lord's favour. Faith in Jesus Christ today means that tomorrow must be different, for me and society. The call of Jesus is universal and personal. We are all called to make a new start. That is the message of the millennium.

'And all eyes in the synagogue were fixed on him.' And ours should be as well.

Cardinal Thomas Winning (2001)
THE CHURCH IN THE THIRD MILLENNIUM

Although I have given much thought to tonight's subject over the past weeks and researched as much as my free time would allow me, I must confess I can't help feeling like Michelangelo as he contemplated his task of decorating the Sistine Chapel. To plot the future of any institution is perilous. To foresee the dangers and areas of likely failure and success, to take every future issue that might affect it into account, is a gigantic task. But when that institution is the Catholic Church, a unique community of divine and human elements and a history of two thousand years, one has a canvas of immense proportions. In the end I might not be satisfied with my contribution, but at least it may offer some points of reflection to you who will participate in the unfolding of the Catholic Church's mission in the twenty-first century.

A very salient point to keep before us when reflecting on the future is this. The future is not merely what has still to come, as if it is detached from the present, a situation out of our control which we must await as passive spectators. Certainly the future will throw up the unexpected, the undesirable and the catastrophic, but, on the whole, the future of an institution like the Church is already being shaped by its current activities. The future can be shaped by us; it is under construction now. We can influence greatly the future of the Church.

We are engaged in an assessment of the Church in the next hundred or so years. We are not playing a game with a crystal ball, prophesying what will happen without backing our claims with good reasons. What the Church is and does today will have a deep bearing on what it does tomorrow. It is a community with a worldwide mission to promote the gospel, the teaching of Jesus

Christ, whose objective is the eternal salvation of the whole human race. What the Church has lived through in the two thousand years of her existence and especially in recent times will have its effect on the Church in the making, just as the history, background and circumstances of you or me have an influence on how we act and who we are seen to be. I suggest that we give some thought to the Church of yesterday and today, dream of the Church of the twenty-first century and try to discern how we get there.

The Church is very much part of the world whether she likes it or not. Because her membership consists of human beings she will have to bear the influences of the world in every age of its history. There have been times when the Church was the dominant institution in that part of the world where she existed. At other times she has been influenced by the world to the detriment of her mission. There is a constant interaction between the Church and the world. However, in our day and really for the first time in history, the Catholic Church is a worldwide institution. It began in the east, but found its centre in the west. Europe has been the foremost continent in the Christianisation of the world. The missionary endeavours of the Church, particularly over the past five hundred years, have seen great geographical advances. Indeed, according to some writers, the centre of gravity of Christendom has shifted to the southern hemisphere: Latin America, Asia, Africa and Oceania. Nowadays, around seventy percent of the world's Catholics are in that part of the world. The consequences of this for the Church of today and tomorrow are immense, and we will deal with these later.

This gigantic extension causes us to confront one great challenge on a worldwide scale, namely the issue of inculturation, which brings us to the nub of the Church's challenge *vis-à-vis* the world in which she has to live. Although the Church may influence culture at certain times, she cannot choose the culture in which she has to live, and her members are certainly influenced by the culture of their time and place. This is such a crucial challenge for the Church in every age that we should reflect for a few moments on what exactly we mean. The culture of a society is its way of life and guide to action passed on from one generation to the next. It comprises the implicit and explicit patterns of behaviour and the world of meaning and understanding in which people live out their lives in a significant manner. It is a way of thinking, feeling, believing, acting. When examining the culture of a society we need to refer to its moral and normative aspects: its ethos. What are the prevailing norms, the things that society rewards, permits, celebrates, prizes, punishes? The ethos of a society is implicit in its way of life, its values, its morality. Culture also includes the world-view of that society, its interpretation of the world, its vision of reality, its concepts therefore of self, nature, life. The culture of a society should be able to answer the great questions every person wishes to pose: Where do we come from? Why are we here? What are we here for? There should be a congruence or a cohesion between society's style of life (its ethos) and its view of reality (world-view). Such congruence gives meaning to lives.

In many societies this synthesis of ethos and world-view is brought about by religion. In the history of the world, religion and religious belief have played a prominent part in the building up of a culture. Today's culture is secular in most areas of the world. This is the Church's biggest challenge. Pope Paul VI, in his post-synodal letter *Evangelii Nuntiandi*, says that the challenge of culture is the most dramatic of our time. This situation did not happen overnight. In the sixteenth and seventeenth centuries the Church suffered setbacks from which she has never fully recovered. The first was the Reformation; the second came around the mid-seventeenth century at the beginning of a period known ironically to us as the Enlightenment. Until about 1650, western society shared a largely homogeneous view of life, faith, tradition and authority. Although by then the Church had become fragmented by the Reformation, the culture was still Christian. By 1650 the whole idea of objective truth came first to be questioned and rejected. Everything, no matter how fundamental or deep-rooted, was up for debate. Old certainties were replaced by new ones, often deriving from the new sciences. As a result, a crippling secularism set in which was ultimately to banish belief in the supernatural from Europe's intellectual culture. A kind of philosophical iconoclasm prevailed, overthrowing everything and anything inherited from the past. Everything had to be based on reason; the foundations of the moral order were undermined. The Enlightenment was a revolution among society's elite, but it soon reached the masses and today underpins all of political and philosophical thought and modern culture.

The secular culture we live in is intensely powerful. The fourth estate – the social communications media – is its prisoner. Modern political thought and the agenda for the future have as their mentors David Hume, Joseph Locke and the other fathers of the Enlightenment. This age is not congenial to religious faith, and that includes, of course, the Christian Church. Over the last thirty years especially, there has been a radical shift – perhaps a landslide would be nearer the mark – in our society's culture. To believe in moral absolutes makes you today a sign of contradiction. That is what the Catholic Church has become. When you have principles of morality you are likely to be 'agin' most of what is happening in the country. When you have no moral principles you can do what you will – and you'll never be against anything. You go with the crowd. Chesterton reminds us that dead things go with the tide. It takes a living thing to swim against the current.

When looking for the areas of shadow and light in the Church today it is essential to remember its *raison d'être*: salvation through closeness to God in this life – holiness. The Church offers the means of holiness – the Word of God, the sacraments, prayer – and holds up models of goodness in every age. She is a mixture of the divine and the human.

The Church over the last century has endured the longest and most severe anti-God persecution ever seen. As it moves into the twenty-first century, the institution most persecuted, the Catholic Church, alone survives while its persecutors in the forms they assumed have all burned out; communism, Nazism, fascism have all disappeared; the Church is still here. Don't forget the Velvet Revolution of 1989. Christians had a big part to play in what is sometimes described in terms of a miracle.

Persecution from now on is unlikely to be physical; the world will no longer stand by idly and watch people die of oppression. No, the persecution of the Church in the future will be much more subtle. It will stem from religious indifference, apathy, and a gradual elimination of religion from public life and policy. The danger is that people who still see a value in religion will be marginalised unless they are prepared to be active in its defence. The 'they' should read 'you and I'. This subtle marginalisation has, as you are aware, already begun. I am convinced that the erosion of Christian values can come from within as well as from without. However, I do not feel defeated or share any sense of despair. The remedies have got to be put in place urgently if the Christian Church is to be a relevant influence in society.

Where do we begin? We could begin at the top and try to produce some masterplan to re-invigorate the Church from the top down. This topic - the question of the central governance of the Catholic Church - certainly seems to take up acres of newsprint. This discussion tends to surround the role of the papacy and the Roman curia. I do not deny for a second that these issues are important. Neither do I deny for a second that the central governance of the Church is likely to undergo some changes in the centuries to come. Collegiality, for example, has to develop. The present Holy Father is anxious to look at how this can come about. His internationalisation of the curia and the college of cardinals is a very evident example of his desire to make sure that the central government of the Church takes account of the worldwide situation, rather than seeing things from a purely Roman viewpoint. Such a move has been widely welcomed and is only just in a Church whose centre of gravity is moving to the southern hemisphere. As for the curia itself, it exists to serve the Pope and the universal Church. That is how it defines itself, and generally that is how it operates. It has a unique insight into the needs of the whole vineyard, an oversight that is not always available to those of us labouring in a particular corner of that vineyard. The Secretariat of State, for example, has a finger on the pulse of the world, and its insights from that special vantage point mean that the Pope is probably the best-informed person in the world. I could expand on this topic further, but I propose to leave it there for this reason: I do not believe that the structures of the Roman curia are a burning issue to the ordinary men and women trying to live out their Catholic faith in the world. Of far greater impact on the lives of most Catholics are the strengths and weaknesses of the local church, both in terms of spiritual leadership and the faith commitment of the laity. And so I would say that the most important locus for the re-invigoration of the Church in the new century lies in the parish.

The parish is in urgent need of spiritual renewal. We have to face up to the fact that there is a yawning gap in the ongoing spiritual formation of adults from the end of their school days onwards. For many practising Catholics, the only vestige of formation they get is in the weekly homily. One generation, in particular, has suffered in this way. I mean the people who are now young parents, but who themselves had their formative years in the turbulence following Vatican II. This generation suffered because religious education text books were too quickly shelved because they seemed to be out of date, but there was nothing to replace them. There was widespread confusion among teachers about what they were expected to teach. This was a wordwide phenomenon. This period of confusion, coinciding, as it did, with the widespread cultural changes of the 1960s and 1970s, means we now have a generation who cannot pass values on to their own children, because their own formation is so weak. This phenomenon, though, is not confined to young people. Sometimes the older generations, too, seem disillusioned about their traditional values and hesitate - in fact, sometimes refuse - to pass them on.

The truth is that at present, even after nearly forty years, we are a Church in transition. Many of the changes in the Church from Vatican II were intended to encourage people to make a knowing and free commitment to the values of the Christian life. The new attitudes repealed many exterior laws and regulations in the hope that the principles underlying them would be internalised. A high degree of moral maturity was thus required and assumed. The response shows that not everyone was ready for that step. Psychologists must have viewed with some apprehension the subsequent amount of changes within a brief space of time. So the Church enters the twenty-first century in a state of transition with some of its members feeling nostalgia for the past and a general sense of fragmentation. Fortunately, the breach caused by some traditionalists under Archbishop Lefebvre seems to be nearing healing.

The predominant image of the Vatican II Church is 'communio' - a community which reaches out and can achieve union with God and the unity of the human race. This image of communion really needs to take root in the local community of the parish. When I say that the parish is in urgent need of renewal, I do not mean that structural changes loom large. Rather, I mean that if the Church wishes to interpret her mission and respond to the needs of a fragmented and much-changed world, she cannot enclose herself in a rigidity of forms, but has to feel herself called to search for better and new ways of proclaiming the good news.

Some of these new forms are visible in the emergence of the new movements in the Church. I read recently in *La Civilta Cattolica* that there are now over sixty of these lay movements recognised by the Church and offering a new dynamism wherever they operate. Many of them try to close the gap in Christian life by offering an effective formation to young adults in the post-school years. These new expressions of Christianity are genuine fruits of the Council and should be seen as such - seen to be complementing, not threatening, the parish and diocesan structures with which we are so familiar. A few years ago I asked the Holy Father why these movements seem to have greater success than the traditional Christian lifestyle. He said: 'I don't know for sure, but I think it is because they are a greater sign of contradiction to the world.' I have often reflected on that. It is true that these movements show a greater sense of the Christian being 'different'. Maybe the rest of us are too keen to go with the tide, not being different enough.

Elsewhere in the world we see other new forms of Christian life emerging. I think of the great insights of the conferences of Latin American bishops at Medéllin and Puebla. It was there, too, that the discernment took place of a liberation theology and the importance of basic Christian communities - another way of being Church which does not threaten or rebel against the diocesan and parish structures, but rather complements them. All over Latin America and Africa we see these groups meeting together to support each other, to study the scriptures, to pray together and to be a living Church in miniature in the heart of the great cities of Latin America and the small villages of southern Africa. Here in Glasgow we are embarking on a similar path, trying to establish small neighbourhood groups who will meet together to reflect on the Word of God and apply that to what is happening in their area - to share faith and then reach out:

faith and action. In this way we aim to build up a community spirit so that the parish becomes a communion of communities.

Whatever the nature or size of a Christian community - be it family, parish, neighbourhood, diocesan or national, or indeed international - there are certain elements which require to be developed to the full. These are: *communio*/community; liturgy and worship; service and witness. The Church of the new century urgently needs to develop all of these areas.

Ever since his election as Bishop of Rome, Pope John Paul II has proclaimed as his life's work a new evangelisation; a new and second effort at proclaiming the good news to the men and women of our time. He says this thrust needs to be new in its fervour, its expression and its strategy. The fervour will be measured by the enthusiasm of the entire Christian family. In other words, a new obligation rests on every baptised member of the Church. This is what the Council called the 'universal call to sanctity and apostolate'. Each person is called upon to be a subject of evangelisation - to evangelise - and also to be the object of evangelisation - to be evangelised and improve their formation.

The new evangelisation is new in its expression because it needs to find new ways of appealing to the man and woman of the new century. The Holy Father covers this in his message for World Communications Day this year, where he gives his *imprimatur*, you might say, to the new technologies of the internet and satellite television as useful tools for the Church to use in getting her message across. The new evangelisation will be new in its strategy because it will require us to develop ever more effective ways of reaching out to people - perhaps learning from the world. I think of the concept of life-long learning as one concept we could profitably import from the secular world, for example. Distance learning is another new possibility for us, as is the erstwhile undreamed of resource that is the internet and email, which offers great potential for spreading the word. Even the children in our primary schools are more aware then we adults are of the Church's vast resources to be found on the internet. Communication is now worldwide and instantaneous. We have to make sure that we are part of this scene or we will always struggle. Now, wherever they are, people can join the Holy Father as he recites the Angelus live every Sunday from Rome or Castel Gandolfo. We can take part, from our own sitting room, in the great events like World Youth Day or the Day of the Family through Catholic television channels broadcasting free by satellite. Equally, via internet, I can read and digest the contents of the Holy Father's message to priests for Holy Thursday at exactly the same time as it is being presented to journalists in Rome. These are great tools we have at our disposal. It is for us to work them into our efforts at evangelisation.

The Church of the new century, besides being a Church of communication – a skill we have never been particularly good at up until our own day – will also be a Church of dialogue. This dialogue extends to civil society, to other world faiths, to Christian denominations, and within the Church herself. (Pope Paul VI covers these in his encyclical *Ecclesiam Suam*.) Love alone opens the way to the truth. And so, the continuing good and open relationships of all who believe in God and those who do not, will help this latter group to see the loving, compassionate and caring face of Christ in us.

I should like to turn now to a central point I feel must be the cornerstone of our efforts in the new century: that is, a rediscovery of the Eucharist, its meaning and its essential role in our lives. Vatican II gave us the beginnings of greater participation in the liturgy, the worship of God and the prayer life of the Church. The last forty years have not been without their problems, of course. Nevertheless, great graces have emerged. A new appreciation with and familiarity with the Word of God is undoubtedly evident in today's Church in a way that was not true before the Council. This allows the kind of faith-sharing groups to develop which I hope will bring about a profound transformation of our communities.

Encouraging young children to pray is now an integral part of every religious lesson in our primary schools. They are learning to pray together, to talk to God, to reflect on the life of Jesus and the saints in a way that is new, and they love it. By praying I don't mean reciting formulae, but rather speaking from the heart. So many of us who have struggled with mental prayer as adults should know that it can be learned far more effectively in childhood. If that capacity for prayer is awakened early it remains with a child throughout life. Of course, prayer cannot be confined to a silent dialogue between the believer and God. To put flesh and blood on this, the Church has always insisted on a regular period of adoration, thanksgiving, repentance and petition. The Church has sought to interpret what Jesus expects of us by insisting on the Sunday Eucharist as a *sine qua non* for every Catholic.

What follows is not a comfortable series of questions, but nevertheless they need to be asked. Could it be that Roman Catholics of today have lost belief in the worship of God? Could it be that the passion, death and resurrection of Jesus Christ mean less and less to them? Could it be that the ordinary rank and file members of the Church need to have their minds refreshed about the meaning of the Eucharist, about the action of the Mass, about the need for the *dies Domini* celebration? If statistics are anything to go by, the answer to each of those questions is yes. I confess to you quite readily that I am concerned that Catholic children in Scotland today are not being encouraged to think of a weekly 'God spot' in their lives. That is why I, and many others involved in the pastoral life of the Church in Scotland, are becoming ever more convinced of the need for a new focus – a new emphasis and catechesis – on the importance of the Sunday Mass in the life of the Christian. Look at the statistics for weekend Mass attendance in any country in Europe.

With the exception of Ireland and Malta, they very seldom rise above 25 percent. In Scotland, the average is around 33 percent – comparatively high, but still pretty awful. It means that two thirds of our Catholics no longer worship with us.

What happens when people deprive themselves of this appointment on a Sunday morning? They cut themselves off from a caring, friendly community of faith who could help them and support them. They cut themselves off from the sacraments and thus the source of grace. They decimate the Christian community and are deprived of its support. They put themselves outside the active, praying family of God. They deny themselves the insights and wisdom of the Word of God. They miss the chance to have their faith developed, either through the homily or through further study or reading, or at least encouragement. They deprive their children of their birthright, their culture and their identity. They leave themselves at the mercy of the latest passing trend and whim of secular society, without any antidote. It is tragically true to say that for many Scots Catholics, the highest act of worship of the Catholic faith – the re-presentation of the sacrifice of Calvary – is simply 'not worth the bother'. When Catholics no longer feel the need to come together to thank God for their lot, Christian life in those communities is at a low ebb.

Of course, the non-attenders are not alone when we apportion blame for this situation. We, their pastoral leaders, are equally culpable. We took it for granted for too long that people would keep coming to Mass on Sunday, that they would regard the Eucharist as the source and summit of the Christian life. We can't take it for granted any more. The re-establishment of the Sunday celebration of the Mass as a norm in the Catholic community therefore needs to be the top priority for the new century.

I believe that the Church of the new century also needs to be a Church of witness. That is why, I believe, the Holy Father is very keen to canonise modern saints – saints who will be role models for the men and women of our time. Perhaps we need modern saints today more than ever. It is when we are hardest hit – as in the sixteenth century – that we as a Church tend to come back to life. That resurrection begins from within, usually through the influence of a few saintly people. At the high point of the Reformation, it is said that there were ten subsequently canonised saints living within a few hundred metres of each other around St Philip Neri's Chiesa Nuova in Rome. We see that pattern of persecution leading to sanctity leading to growth even in our own day as we read accounts of the lives of martyrs like Edith Stein and Maximilian Kolbe, the stories of the Spanish Civil War martyrs, or the victims of communist persecution in eastern Europe. And so, learning from history, I look to the new century to be also a century of saints. The last time I visited the Congregation for the Causes of Saints in Rome, I heard that there are two thousand people on the list waiting to be beatified or canonised, and most of them are lay-people – so take heart!

By a century of saints I mean a century in which Christians will take seriously the priesthood of all the baptised, the universal call to holiness, and the need to read the signs of their times. Such a vibrant Christianity may produce one or two great prophetic figures. On the other hand, it may produce a myriad of 'little prophets' – men and women who know how to show by the way they live their lives that Jesus Christ is alive in his Church and his world – yesterday, today and forever. Both are needed – the great prophetic voices like the Holy Father's, and the small, hidden apostolate of so many saints of everyday life who know how to achieve a heroic degree of sanctity in their everyday activities in the office, the shop, the factory, or the home. If enough of these saints of the new century emerge, then I believe the new springtime of evangelisation dreamed of by Blessed John XXIII at the convocation of the Council, may soon dawn.

It is fascinating to speculate about the Church's mission in the years to come. Much will depend on the kind of leadership the Church enjoys. But before we reflect on leadership, it is important to note that there are many areas of present concern which are not likely to disappear while this century is still young. I am thinking about the shortage of priests and the lack of any stable pattern of vocations to the priesthood. The many factors which go to make this a real concern are not going to go away unless there is a radical shift in society's attitudes. One factor which is frequently overlooked is the birthrate which continues to decline all over Europe. Fewer people means fewer vocations, and we are going to have to get used to the idea that we are unlikely to have a community of priests in many parishes. There is always potential in every problem, of course. The laity, if hitherto unwilling, might well be forced by circumstances to play a more active role in the life of the parish. The fact that many may have to travel some distance to Mass on a Sunday is generally made more feasible because of the growing numbers of people who either own or have access to a car. Parishes may have to close. And we need to answer the question, 'Did we ever really need all the church buildings we presently have?'

The priestly life and ministry will come up for discussion. Must all Catholic priests be celibate, for instance? That question has been answered, although by way of exception, by the fact that there are many married ex-Anglican priests who are now Catholic priests in the active ministry. But the question continues to be asked: should celibacy go? One of the characteristics of our society is the desire for endless change. The mood is, if it's changeable, let's experiment. But in a world that is sex-mad, or being made to see everything in terms of sexuality, is there to be no room for a lifestyle which reminds people that sexual activity can be sacrificed for a greater good? Is it not important to remind people that family life can be surrendered so as to be a sign that there is something higher than this present life?

At a time when there is great turbulence about sex and all its implications, is this really the best time to abandon the celibate life freely accepted and offered for the kingdom of God?

Another area of turbulence is the future of religious life. Here I think we can see present trends in an unduly negative way. Of course, we have to ask ourselves what will be the future for many religious communities and congregations in the face of fewer vocations. We certainly see a great fall in the numbers of those taking up religious life. On the face of it, it seems not so good. But we need to take account of the previous relative abundance. Religious congregations and people devoting themselves to certain sacred causes have always arisen in response to the needs of the Church and the age. Over the last two hundred years or so, education was a clamant need; care of the sick was another; care of the poor, the homeless. Thousands of young men and women gave their lives for these causes. To a great extent these needs are all taken care of now in other ways, mainly through the welfare state. In the past, the number of people entering the religious life was higher than today because the needs were greater. Today the need is for witness in the market place – where the action is. The universal call to holiness of Vatican II implied that, fine though it is, you need not enter the cloister to be holy. The laity are called to witness in temporal society, to reach places others cannot reach. Hence the growth in the new religious movements I mentioned earlier.

Much of the future of the Church in the new century will depend on the calibre of leadership it enjoys, and I mean leadership from the laity - that sleeping giant - as well as from the clergy. The laity need to be offered the space to exercise their charisms in the Church. We need to do this more effectively and with greater urgency. There are certain characteristics of leadership which must be taken into account. A leader needs to challenge; to inspire a shared vision; to enable others to act; to model the way forward; and to encourage the heart. Pope John Paul has given and continues to give us this kind of leadership. In his most recent letter to the Church at the end of the holy year and the start of the new millennium, *Novo Millennio Ineunte*, he urges us, '*Duc in altum*', cast out into the deep - that is where the fish are. I would translate this as, 'Take the plunge'.

Before I end, let me sum up how I would hope the Church of the new century will be in four words: living, free, courageous, and involved. Living because she will continue to confront the men and women of the new century with a coherent and vibrant message which makes moral and intellectual demands on them, demands which produce good fruits; fruits of love and compassion and solidarity and faith. Free because never before has the Church been more free of the shackles of temporal power than she is today. Freed from these golden shackles, she can make her voice heard loudly and clearly, even in the face of worldly power. Courageous because the Church will increasingly be called to be a sign of contradiction to society and all it holds dear. That means the Church must be prepared to face down the values of this world, and denounce oppression, immorality, sin and its structures, even when doing so earns a crown of martyrdom - literal or metaphorical. And involved because the Church purified will be a Church at the heart of the world - involved in the day to day struggles of all peoples, especially the marginalised, those without a voice and those who are excluded. This is the Church of the future that I can begin to see emerging: a purified Church; a renewed Church; a brave Church; a humble Church.

I should like to leave you tonight with words which I often cite, words of inspiration: In this world of change, we must neither live nor work in a past which no longer exists, nor in the present which is running away from us. If we plan the future, we must begin now.

Bishop James Sangu, 'Justice in the African context'
Briefing vol 5 issue 30, 17 October 1975

Bishop Alan Clark, 'Ecumenism – the growing point of unity'
Briefing vol 8 issue 40, 23 November 1978

Bishop Cahal Daly, 'Northern Ireland – from impasse to initiative'
Briefing vol 9 issues 32 & 33, 7 & 14 September 1979

Cardinal Johannes Willebrands, 'Is Christianity anti-Semitic?'
Briefing vol 15 issue 6, 22 March 1985

Cardinal Joseph Ratzinger, 'Consumer materialism and Christian hope'
Briefing vol 18 issue 3, 5 February 1988

Archbishop Derek Worlock, 'What the Butler did not see – the changing face of education'
Briefing vol 25 special education issue, June 1995

Cardinal Cahal Daly, 'The Church's magisterium in face of the moral crisis of our time'
Briefing vol 27 special Linacre Centre issue, October 1997

Cardinal Basil Hume OSB, 'Jesus Christ today'
Briefing vol 29 special Cardinal Hume issue, July 1999

Cardinal Thomas Winning, 'The Church in the third millennium'
Briefing vol 31 issue 6, 13 June 2001

THE SEARCH FOR CHRISTIAN UNITY

The Search for Christian Unity - approved by the Bishops' Conference of England and Wales - is a popular version of the Vatican's *Directory for the Application of Principles and Norms on Ecumenism*.

Chapter 1, 'The search for Christian unity', makes the Catholic Church's ecumenical commitment very clear.

Chapter 2, 'Organisation in the Catholic Church at the service of Christian unity', describes how the Church officially structures its search for unity.

Chapter 3, 'Ecumenical formation in the Catholic Church', deals with the vital issue of learning about ecumenism and forming an ecumenical attitude.

Chapter 4, 'Communion in life and spiritual activity among the baptised', spells out appropriate ways of sharing in prayer and in both sacramental and non-sacramental worship.

Chapter 5, 'Ecumenical co-operation, dialogue and common witness', looks at practical details of working, witnessing and sharing in dialogue together.

The Search for Christian Unity includes study questions and points for action, and a foreword by Cardinal Cormac Murphy-O'Connor.

The Search for Christian Unity, A5, 80 pages, £4.00, ISBN 0 905241 21 5.

A SPIRITUALITY OF WORK

A Spirituality of Work, produced by the Committee for the World of Work of the Bishops' Conference of England and Wales, brings together prayers and Church teachings on work.

Chapter 1, 'Work in the sacred scriptures', examines the place of human work in God's plan since the beginning.

Chapter 2, 'The Church's teaching on work', outlines the development of the Church's teaching on work, particularly as expressed in the Second Vatican Council and in the writings of the modern popes.

Chapter 3, 'Human dignity and the value of work', explores this further, in the context of human dignity and the wider society.

The fourth chapter provides prayers and meditations for individuals and for use in groups and church services, and a final section is a list of further Catholic resources.

A Spirituality of Work, A5, 52 pages, £2.50, ISBN 0 905241 18 5.

SUBSTANCE MISUSE TODAY: A CATHOLIC REFLECTION

Substance Misuse Today: A Catholic Reflection, produced by the Social Welfare Committee of the Bishops' Conference of England and Wales, outlines how the Church might respond, both as a whole and locally, to the problem of drugs and alcohol misuse.

Substance Misuse Today covers the spiritual aspects of addiction, social context, drugs prevention, parish and family support, education and treatment, crime and prisons, sport and image. It also provides practical guidance for those approached by addicts, and an appendix of useful contacts.

Substance Misuse Today: A Catholic Reflection, A4, 52 pages, £3.00, ISBN 0 905241 16 9.

THE PRIORITY OF ADULT FORMATION

The Priority of Adult Formation - from the Bishops' Conference Committee for Catechesis and Adult Christian Education - charts the development in the Church's understanding of adult learning. Drawing on the *Catechism of the Catholic Church* and the *General Directory for Catechesis*, it examines how the Church has taught about formation, what the present situation is, and the way forward, in the context of the Church's mission to evangelise.

The Priority of Adult Formation, A5, 36 pages, £1.00, ISBN 0 905241 17 7.

150 YEARS

150 Years - the official souvenir book for the 150th anniversary of the Restoration of the Hierarchy of England and Wales.

In full colour, this book includes the anniversary celebrations, papal message, the original papal letter of 1850, an article on the Restoration, chronology of events, photographs, and more.

150 Years, A4, 92 pages, £5.00.

BRIEFING

Briefing is the official monthly journal of the Catholic Bishops' Conferences of Great Britain. It contains documents, information and news from the Church in Britain, Rome and overseas; official documents from the official sources.

£29.50 annual subscription.

Publications available from
Catholic Bishops' Conference of England and Wales
39 Eccleston Square   London SW1V 1BX